W9-BZP-135

Science, Technology, and Society

The Impact
of Science
in the
20th Century

Science, Technology, and Society

The Impact of Science in the 20th Century

Phillis Engelbert, Editor

VOLUME 2

Mathematics

Medicine

THOMSON

GALE

Detroit • New York • San Diego • San Francisco • Cleveland • New Haven, Conn. • Waterville, Maine • London • Munich

Science, Technology, and Society: The Impact of Science in the 20th Century

Phillis Engelbert

Project Editor
Diane Sawinski

Permissions
Shalice Shah-Caldwell

Imaging and Multimedia
Robert Duncan, Robyn Young

Product Design
Tracey Rowens

Composition
Evi Seoud

Manufacturing
Rita Wimberley

LIBRARY OF CONGRESS CATALOGING-IN-PUBLICATION DATA

Science, technology, and society : the impact of science in the 20th century / Phillis Engelbert, editor.

p. cm.

Summary: Examines scientific discoveries and developments within their historic context, showing how social trends and events influenced science and how scientific developments changed people's lives. Includes bibliographical references and index.

ISBN 0-7876-5649-6 (set) 1. Science—History—20th century. 2. Science—Social aspects—History—20th century. 3. Science and civilization—History—20th century. 4. Technology—History—20th century. 5. Technology—Social aspects—History—20th century. 6. Technology and civilization—History—20th century. [1. Science—History—20th century. 2. Science—Social aspects. 3. Science and civilization. 4. Technology—History—20th century. 5. Technology—Social aspects. 6. Technology and civilization.] I. Engelbert, Phillis.

Q125 .S395 2002   2002004668
509.04—dc21

0-7876-5650-X (volume 1)   0-7876-5651-8 (volume 2)   0-7876-5652-6 (volume 3)

Printed in the United States of America
10 9 8 7 6 5 4 3 2 1

Contents

VOLUME 1

chapter one   # Life Science

Contents

VOLUME 2

chapter two Mathematics

Contents

chapter three ## Medicine

Contents
_____

VOLUME 3

chapter four   Physical Science

Technology

Reader's Guide

Advances in science and technology in the twentieth century, more so than in any previous century, dramatically changed the daily lives of virtually all the world's inhabitants. Early in the century, scientists identified genes as the units of heredity, and by the end of the century they had learned how to manipulate genes in order to introduce new traits in organisms. The field of medicine, with the development of vaccines and antibiotics, saw more progress during the twentieth century than during the previous two thousand years combined. In addition, the mass production of automobiles expanded possibilities for working and vacationing, and the invention of the airplane and the computer ushered in worldwide travel and communication. The twentieth century is also known as the space age, for the development of spacecraft, and the atomic age, for the splitting of the atom and the construction of nuclear power reactors and nuclear weapons.

Science, Technology, and Society: The Impact of Science in the 20th Century is designed to help students understand the impact that twentieth-century discoveries and inventions had on the course of human history. Scientific advances are examined within their historical context, showing how social trends and events influenced science and how scientific developments changed people's lives. The benefits and drawbacks of scientific and technological developments are objectively examined, encouraging critical thinking.

Format

Science, Technology, and Society: The Impact of Science in the 20th Century is divided into five chapters across three volumes. The Life Science chapter appears in Volume One. The Mathematics and Medicine chapters appear in Volume Two. And the Physical Science and Technology chapters appear in Volume Three. The following sections appear in each chapter:

Chronology: A timeline of key events within the chapter's discipline.

Overview: A summary of the scientific discoveries and developments, trends, and issues within the discipline.

Essays: Topical essays describing major discoveries and developments within the discipline and relating them to social history. Information in the essays is divided under the standard rubrics Overview, Background, and Impact.

Biographies: Biographical profiles providing personal background on important individuals within the discipline, and often introducing students to additional important issues in science and society in the twentieth century.

Brief Biographies: Brief biographical mentions introducing students to the major accomplishments of other notable scientists, researchers, teachers, and inventors important within the discipline.

Research and Activity Ideas: Offering students ideas for reports, presentations, or classroom activities related to the topics discussed in the chapter.

For More Information: Providing sources for further research on the topics and individuals discussed in the chapter.

Other features

Sidebars in every chapter highlight interesting events, issues, or individuals related to the subject. Nearly 180 black-and-white photographs help illustrate the discoveries and the individuals who made them. In addition, cross-references to subjects discussed in other topic essays are indicated with "see references" in parenthesis, while cross-references to individuals discussed elsewhere in the title are indicated by boldface type and "see references" in parenthesis. Each volume concludes with a cumulative subject index so that students can easily locate the people, places, and events discussed throughout *Science, Technology, and Society: The Impact of Science in the 20th Century.*

Special thanks

Special thanks are due to Ken Plochinski, Visiting Professor of Mathematics at the University of Michigan in Ann Arbor, Michigan, for his assistance with the mathematics chapter.

Comments and Suggestions

We welcome your comments on *Science, Technology, and Society: The Impact of Science in the 20th Century* and suggestions for other science topics to consider. Please write: Editors, *Science, Technology, and Society: The Impact of Science in the 20th Century,* U•X•L, 27500 Drake Rd., Farmington Hills, Michigan 48331-3535; call toll-free: 1-800-877-4253; fax to (248) 414-5043; or send e-mail via http://www.gale.com.

Chronology

1903   American inventors Wilbur Wright and Orville Wright accomplish the first sustained flight in a gasoline-engine-powered airplane.

1905   The word "gene" is introduced by Danish botanist Wilhelm L. Johannsen to describe a unit of heredity.

1905   German-born American physicist Albert Einstein pens the special theory of relativity, which states that for bodies in constant motion (that is, not speeding up or slowing down), time and space change depending on the position of the observer.

1906   Spanish anatomist Santiago Ramon y Cajal wins the Nobel Prize in physiology or medicine for determining that the brain is made up of independent nerve cells (neurons), and is not a continuous net as previously believed.

1907   Belgian-American chemist Leo Hendrik Baekeland produces Bakelite, the first completely synthetic plastic.

1912   German astronomer and meteorologist Alfred Wegener presents the theory of continental drift, the idea that all continents had

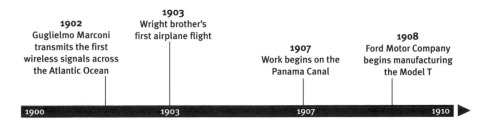

1902
Guglielmo Marconi transmits the first wireless signals across the Atlantic Ocean

1903
Wright brother's first airplane flight

1907
Work begins on the Panama Canal

1908
Ford Motor Company begins manufacturing the Model T

1900   1903   1907   1910

once been part of a single, original landmass gradually drifting apart to their present locations.

1913 American industrialist Henry Ford increases the efficiency of the assembly line by installing a conveyor belt at his Dearborn, Michigan, Model T plant.

1915 German-born American physicist Albert Einstein authors the general theory of relativity, which explains that gravity is the result of curved space-time.

1918 Norwegian meteorologist Jacob Bjerknes establishes the concept of fronts, which are dividing lines between adjacent air masses along which storms form.

1925 The Tennessee state government passes the Butler Act, making it illegal to teach "any theory that denies the story of the Divine Creation of man as taught in the Bible, and to teach instead that man has descended from a lower order of animals."

1928 Scottish medical doctor Alexander Fleming discovers that bread mold produces the chemical substance penicillin, the first antibiotic used to fight infection.

1933 Hungarian-American biochemist Albert Szent-Györgyi discovers vitamin C, for which he will be awarded the Nobel Prize in physiology or medicine in 1937.

1936 The Hoover Dam, which at 726 feet (221 meters) in height is the tallest concrete arch dam in the United States, is completed.

1937 British mathematician Alan M. Turing writes "On Computable Numbers," in which he describes a theoretical computer that operates according to a set of instructions and provides a blueprint for the modern digital computer.

1938 Wallace Hume Carothers, a researcher at DuPont Chemical Company, invents the synthetic fiber nylon.

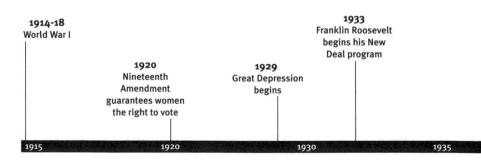

1914-18
World War I

1920
Nineteenth
Amendment
guarantees women
the right to vote

1929
Great Depression
begins

1933
Franklin Roosevelt
begins his New
Deal program

1915   1920   1930   1935

1938   Russian-American physicist Vladimir Zworykin displays his electronic television system at the New York World's Fair.

1940   Australian-English pathologist Howard Florey and German biochemist Ernst Chain purify penicillin for human use.

1941   President Franklin Delano Roosevelt gives the order to begin the Manhattan Project, the secret U.S. effort to construct atomic weapons during World War II (1939–45).

1942   Italian-American physicist Enrico Fermi constructs the world's first nuclear reactor at the University of Chicago.

1943   The first American computer, the enormous Mark I, is unveiled at Harvard University.

1944   Hungarian-born American mathematician John von Neumann and German-born American economist Oskar Morgenstern apply game theory to economic competition in their classic book *Theory of Games and Economic Behavior.*

1946   The first electronic computer in the United States, the ENIAC (Electronic Numerical Integrator and Computer), is completed.

1948   The World Health Organization is founded as an international public health agency of the United Nations; its mission is to attain for all people "the highest possible level of health."

1954   American microbiologist Jonas Salk develops the first vaccine for polio.

1960   The U.S. Food and Drug Administration (FDA) approves for use the birth control pill, which is the first safe, easily used, and reliable contraceptive.

Early 1960s   New Math, a method of teaching mathematics that stresses conceptual (intuitive) understanding of the foundations of mathematics, is launched in the United States.

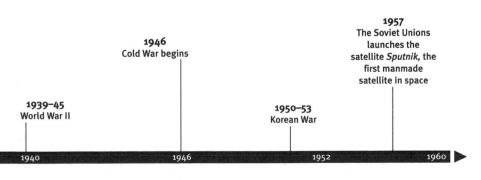

1957
The Soviet Unions launches the satellite *Sputnik,* the first manmade satellite in space

1946
Cold War begins

1939–45
World War II

1950–53
Korean War

1940   1946   1952   1960

1962 American geologist Harry Hess (1906–1969) publishes *History of Ocean Basins,* a document that offers proof for plate tectonics, the theory that Earth's crust is composed of rigid plates that "float" toward or away from each other.

1962 NASA's *Mariner 2* is launched and heads for Venus, becoming the first interplanetary space probe.

1962 Rachel Carson publishes *Silent Spring,* a book that warns the public of the dangers of pesticide use.

1964 Cigarettes and other tobacco products are conclusively linked to lung cancer in a landmark report by Surgeon General Luther Terry titled *Smoking and Health: Report of the Advisory Committee to the Surgeon General of the Public Health Service.*

1968 South African surgeon Christiaan Barnard performs the world's first successful human heart transplant.

1968 The U.S. Supreme Court declares that state laws banning the teaching of evolution in public schools are unconstitutional.

1970 The Environmental Protection Agency (EPA) is created by executive order of President Richard Nixon.

1972 Evidence that evolution did not always occur in a smooth and gradual manner, but that there have been long periods of very slow change punctuated with bursts of extremely rapid speciation, is offered by American paleontologist Stephen Jay Gould.

1973 The first successful tests of genetic engineering are conducted by American biochemists Stanley N. Cohen and Herbert W. Boyer, when they insert DNA fragments into the bacterium *Escherichia coli* (*E. coli*).

1973 British economist E. F. Schumacher writes *Small Is Beautiful: Economics As If People Mattered,* advocating production using local resources to increase the well-being of the local populace.

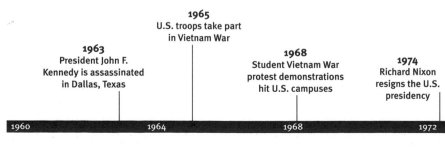

1963
President John F. Kennedy is assassinated in Dallas, Texas

1965
U.S. troops take part in Vietnam War

1968
Student Vietnam War protest demonstrations hit U.S. campuses

1974
Richard Nixon resigns the U.S. presidency

1960   1964   1968   1972

1976 The Apple I, the first fully assembled personal computer, is offered for sale.

1980 American physicist Luis Alvarez and his geologist son Walter Alvarez find high levels of iridium, an element contained in meteorites, in a layer of clay-rich rock deposited 65 million years ago, supporting the theory that a meteorite wiped out the dinosaurs.

1981 AIDS is officially recognized as a disease by the U.S. Centers for Disease Control (CDC).

1984 American researcher Robert Gallo and French virologist Luc Montagnier discover the human immunodeficiency virus (HIV), the retrovirus that causes AIDS. Gallo develops a blood test to detect the presence of HIV.

1986 The worst nuclear power accident in history occurs at the Chernobyl nuclear power plant in Ukraine, in the former Soviet Union.

1991 British physicist Tim Berners-Lee introduces the World Wide Web, an interface providing access to countless pages of information on the Internet.

1993 British mathematician Andrew Wiles offers a proof for history's most famous unsolved mathematical problem: Fermat's last theorem.

1994 American mathematician John Forbes Nash is awarded a Nobel Prize for economics in 1994 for his work on noncooperative game theory.

2000 Ninety-eight percent of American households possess at least one television set, and 41 percent of American households own three or more.

2000 The Human Genome Project (HGP) is completed five years ahead of schedule. It provides a blueprint for humanity by describing the location and details of every gene on every chromosome.

2001 The number of people globally living with HIV or AIDS is estimated at 36 million.

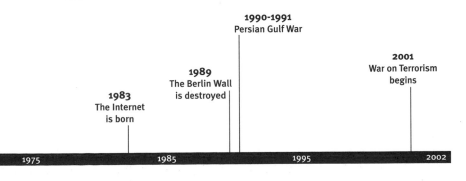

1990-1991
Persian Gulf War

2001
War on Terrorism begins

1989
The Berlin Wall is destroyed

1983
The Internet is born

1975   1985   1995   2002

Words to Know

A

Acid rain: rain that is made more acidic due to industrial processes that place sulfuric and/or nitric acid in the air.

Air mass: a large quantity of air throughout which temperature and moisture content are fairly constant.

Air pollutant: any harmful substance that exists in the atmosphere at concentrations great enough to endanger the health of living organisms.

Air pressure: the pressure exerted by the weight of air over a given area of Earth's surface; also called atmospheric pressure or barometric pressure.

Aircraft: any machine that travels by air, whether it is engine-powered or gets its lift from buoyant air (such as hot air or hydrogen gas).

Airplane: engine-powered, heavier-than-air, winged aircraft.

Airship: engine-powered craft that is lighter than air; also called a dirigible.

Allele: one of two or more forms a gene may take.

Altruism: the practice of sacrificing one's own interest for the benefit of others.

Antibiotics: class of drugs that fight infections caused by bacteria.

Appropriate technology: tools and techniques that are small-scale, locally controlled, environmentally sustainable, and beneficial to the local population.

Artificial selection: technique of plant breeding in which humans select plants with desirable traits and facilitate the reproduction of only those plants.

Asteroid: a rocky chunk of matter in orbit around the Sun.

B

Bakelite: early form of plastic that is hard, clear, and water-resistant.

Balloon: lighter-than-aircraft that consists of large fabric bag (called an envelope) filled with hot air, hydrogen gas, or helium gas. Hanging beneath the envelope is a basket (called a gondola).

Beriberi: a disease caused by a deficiency of thiamine and characterized by nerve and gastrointestinal disorders.

Big bang theory: the theory that explains the beginning of the universe as a tremendous explosion from a single point that occurred fifteen to twenty billion years ago.

Biodiversity: the wide range of organisms, plants and animals, that exist within any given geographical region.

Bioengineering: also called genetic engineering, it is the process of manipulating specific genes of an organism in order to improve the traits that the organism will pass on to its offspring.

Biotechnology: use of biological organisms, systems, or processes to make or modify products.

Biplane: airplane or glider with two sets of wings, one above the other.

Bomber: airplane used in war that is outfitted with cannons and machine guns.

Brain: the mass of nerve tissue located in the head that controls the body's functions; it is the part of the central nervous system that receives and transmits impulses.

Brain stem: the stalk of the brain; it is continuous with the spinal column.

C

Cable television: system of delivering television transmissions through coaxial cables, insulated tubes of electrically conducting material.

Calvin cycle: sequence of dark reactions in photosynthesis that use the high-energy compounds produced in light reactions to make carbohydrates.

Cancer: a disease characterized by the uncontrolled multiplication of abnormal cells within the body.

Carcinogen: a cancer-causing agent.

Cathode ray tube: device through which electrons are rapidly scanned, creating patterns of moving light on a fluorescent screen; the earliest television picture tube.

Celluloid: early form of hard, flexible plastic that is today used in ping-pong balls.

Central nervous system: the portion of the nervous system that consists of the brain and spinal cord.

Cerebellum: the bottom rear part of the brain that coordinates movement.

Cerebrum: the folded mass of nerve cells that sits over the rest of the brain and coordinates voluntary movements.

Chemosynthesis: the process of making food using the energy derived from chemical reactions.

Chemotherapy: the use of powerful chemicals to kill cancer cells in the human body.

Chlorophyll: a green pigment found in plants that absorbs sunlight, providing the energy used in photosynthesis.

Chloroplast: a small structure in a plant cell that contains chlorophyll and in which the process of photosynthesis takes place.

Chromosome: a structure that organizes genetic information in the nucleus of a cell.

Clean Air Act: set of environmental regulations (limiting pollutants emitted by cars, factories, and other sources) first enacted by the U.S. Congress in 1970 and updated several times since then.

Cloning: technique of genetic engineering in which an offspring is produced asexually (without joining egg and sperm) that has the exact same genes as its donor organism.

Cold front: the line behind which a cold air mass is advancing and in front of which a warm air mass is retreating.

Computed tomography (CT) scanning: an X-ray technique in which a three-dimensional image of a body part is put together by computer using a series of X-ray pictures taken from different angles along a straight line; often called computerized axial tomography (CAT).

Computer: electronic machine that can receive, process, store, and display information. It carries out a range of mathematical and logical functions at great speeds.

Computer hardware: physical and electronic parts of a computer system, including central processing unit, disk drive, monitor, keyboard, mouse, and printer.

Computer memory: the part of the computer that stores programs and other information.

Computer program: set of step-by-step instructions, similar to a recipe, that tells a computer what to do; also called computer software.

Conservation: the act of using natural resources in a way that ensures that they will be available to future generations.

Continental drift: geologic theory proposed by German scientist Alfred Wegener that all continents were part of a single, original landmass before they slowly separated and gradually drifted apart.

Convergence: the movement of air inward, toward a central point.

Cosmology: the study of the origin, evolution, and structure of the universe.

Creation science: the use of modern scientific methods to verify religious truths of the Bible.

Creationism: a belief in the biblical, Christian account of how God created the universe and all living things; specifically that God created Earth within the six-day period described in Genesis (the first book of the Bible).

Crust: outermost layer of Earth, varying in thickness from 3.5 50 miles (5 to 80 kilometers).

Cyberspace: the computer universe including software and data.

Cyclogenesis: the process by which an extratropical storm is formed.

Cyclone: a weather system in which winds spiral counterclockwise around a low-pressure area; also called a storm.

D

Dam: barrier built across a river or stream that blocks and controls the flow of water.

Diagnostic: pertaining to the identification of a diseased condition.

DNA (deoxyribonucleic acid): large, complex molecules found in the nuclei of cells that carries genetic information for an organism's development.

Dominant trait: a trait that is expressed when inherited from one parent.

E

Earthquake: a sudden shifting of masses of rock beneath Earth's surface that releases enormous amounts of energy and sends out shock waves that cause the ground to shake.

Ecosystem: community of plants and animals and their physical surroundings.

Electric generator: machine in which a magnet is turned through a coil of wire and produces electricity.

Electric vehicles: vehicles that run on electric motors instead of gasoline-powered engines.

Electromagnetic radiation: the range of wavelengths produced by the interaction of electricity and magnetism.

Electronics: branch of science dealing with the flow of electricity through a vacuum, gases, or semiconductors. Electronic devices are used to process and store information, accurately and efficiently.

Endemic disease: disease that normally occurs in a population at a relatively constant rate.

Environmental Protection Agency (EPA): government agency, created in 1970, to monitor and enforce the environmental policies of the federal government.

Environmentalism: the movement to preserve and improve the natural environment, and particularly to control pollution.

Enzyme: biological molecule, usually a protein, that promotes a biochemical reaction but is not consumed by the reaction.

Epidemic disease: disease with a rapid increase in the rate of infection.

Epidemilogy: the medical discipline concerned with epidemic diseases.

Ethics: moral principles or values governing a particular culture or group.

Ethology: the scientific and objective study of the behavior of animals in the wild rather than in captivity.

Eugenics: the study of improving the human race by selective breeding (the deliberate pairing of individuals with desirable traits so they can pass on those traits to future generations).

Evolution: the theory that all plants and animals developed gradually from earlier forms over a long period of time and that variations within a species are the result of adaptive traits passed on from generation to generation.

Evolutionary psychology: the scientific study of the evolutionary significance of human behavior.

Exaptation: any adapted trait that performs a beneficial function different from the one it originally evolved to serve.

F

Fermentation: chemical reaction in which enzymes break down complex organic compounds (for example, carbohydrates and sugars) into simpler ones (for example, ethyl alcohol).

Fossil fuels: coal, oil, and natural gas; materials composed of the remains of plants or animals that covered Earth millions of years ago and are today burned for fuel.

Front: the dividing line between two air masses.

Fuel cells: devices that generate electricity by combining hydrogen and oxygen; they emit water vapor as a by-product.

G

Game: a situation in which a conflict arises between two or more players.

Game theory: the branch of mathematics concerned with the analysis of conflict situations; it provides a model for understanding and predicting behavior of rivals in situations where the participants are driven by a mixture of interests and goals.

Games of incomplete information: games such as poker, in which players make decisions without full knowledge about the various elements of the game.

Gene: a segment of a DNA (deoxyribonucleic acid) molecule contained in the nucleus of a cell that acts as a kind of code for the production of some specific protein. Genes carry instructions for the formation, functioning, and transmission of specific traits from one generation to another.

Gene therapy: experimental technique involving the alteration of human genes to cure certain genetic disorders.

General theory of relativity: the theory in which German-born American physicist Albert Einstein demonstrated that gravity is the result of curved space-time.

Genetics: a branch of biology that deals with inheritance in living organisms.

Genetic determinism: the theory that social behaviors are the products of genetically determined instincts.

Genetic engineering: the process of manipulating specific genes of an organism to produce or improve a product or to analyze the genes.

Genome: genetic material of a human being; the complete genetic structure of a species.

Genotype: the genetic information that a living thing inherits from its parents that affects its makeup, appearance, and function.

Geology: the study of the origin, history, and structure of Earth.

Germ theory of disease: the belief that disease is caused by germs (microorganisms).

Glider: motorless airplane that rides on wind currents.

Global warming: the theory that average temperatures around the world have begun to rise, and will continue to rise, due to an increase of certain gases, called greenhouse gases, in the atmosphere; also called enhanced greenhouse effect.

Gravity: the force of attraction between objects, the strength of which depends on the mass of each object and the distance between them.

Group selection: the theory that selfless behavior and cooperation benefit a group (family, tribe, or nation) in its struggle for existence.

H

Hereditary: traits that are passed on, or are capable of being passed on, through genetic material from parents to offspring.

High-definition television (HDTV): method of television transmission that uses twice the number of scan lines as standard television and a larger number of pixels, resulting in an extremely sharp image and a three-dimensional effect.

Hybrid: the offspring of parents from two different species.

Hybrid vehicles: vehicles that run on more than one source of power, such as gasoline and electricity.

Hybridization: the production of offspring from two parents (such as plants, animals, or cells) of different breeds, species, or varieties.

Hydroelectric power plant: facility at which the energy of the moving water is converted into electricity.

Hydrothermal vents: cracks in the ocean floor through which highly acidic, extremely hot water is released into the ocean.

I

Integrated circuit (IC): thumbnail-sized piece of semiconductor material, usually silicon, that holds millions of transistors and other electronic components; also called silicon chip, microchip, or chip.

Intelligent design theory: school of thought that accepts that Earth is billions of years old, but suggests that a divine force, or "intelligent designer," and not natural selection, drives evolution.

Internet: a vast computerized information system that links millions of computer terminals around the world in a web of networks and shared software.

Irradiation: the process of exposing food to low doses of radiation to reduce contamination and spoilage in food.

Isotope: (see radioactive isotope entry)

J

Jet engine: type of airplane engine in which compressed air enters a combustion chamber, is mixed with fuel, and ignites and burns rapidly. This causes the expulsion of hot, high-pressure air through the rear of the chamber, which thrusts the airplane forward.

Jet streams: narrow bands of fast winds that zip through the top of the troposphere in a west-to-east direction at high speeds.

K

K-T boundary: the rock layer containing high levels of iridium that was deposited sixty-five million years ago, at the end of Cretaceous (K) period and the beginning of the Tertiary (T) period.

L

Lamarckism: theory that characteristics acquired during an organism's lifetime, through habit or use (or lost through disuse), could be passed on to succeeding generations.

Lift: the force that causes aircraft to fly; it may be provided by buoyant, lighter-than-air gas in a balloon or by the movement of air over the wings of an airplane or glider.

M

Magnetic resonance imaging (MRI): process of subjecting a sample of material to a strong magnetic field and radio waves and observing the response of the atoms in that sample; it is used to produce detailed, three-dimensional computer images of body tissues and organs.

Mammography: X-ray visualization of breast tissue.

Manhattan Project: the secret U.S. government project to build an atomic weapon during World War II (1939–45).

Mantle: thick, dense layer of rock that lies beneath Earth's crust. The mantle is about 1,800 miles (2,900 kilometers) thick and accounts for about 84 percent of Earth's volume.

Mass: the total amount of matter in an object.

Mean: a measure of central tendency found by adding all of the numbers in a set and dividing by the number of numbers.

Median: the middle value in a set of measurements when those measurements are arranged in sequence from least to greatest.

Meteorite: a chunk of rock and/or metal that has broken off a larger space object, such as an asteroid or a comet, and falls to Earth's surface.

Meteorology: the scientific study of the atmosphere and atmospheric processes, namely weather and climate.

Mid-ocean ridge: a several-thousand-mile-long strip of ocean floor along which tectonic plates (large sections of Earth's crust) are pulling away from one another.

Minimax theorem: the central theorem of game theory. It states that for any zero-sum, two-player game there is a strategy that leads to a solution in which each player guarantees their maximum payoff and one player's expected gain will exactly equal the other's expected loss.

Mode: the value that occurs most frequently in any set of measurements.

Modem: a device that converts computer signals into a form that can be carried through telephone lines, and converts telephone signals into a form that can be recognized by computer; abbreviated form of modulate and demodulate.

Mutation: any permanent change in hereditary material, involving either a physical change in chromosome relations or a biochemical change in genes.

N

Nash equilibrium: a solution for noncooperative games, proposed by American mathematician John Forbes Nash, that provides a way for all players' expectations to be fulfilled and strategies optimized.

Natural selection: also known as survival of the fittest; the natural process by which those organisms best adapted to their environment survive and pass their traits to offspring.

Nerve: a bundle of fibers in the central nervous system that relay sensory stimuli and motor impulses.

Nervous system: the bodily system that in vertebrates is made up of the brain and spinal cord, nerves, ganglia, and other organs and that receives and interprets stimuli and transmits impulses to targeted organs.

Network: a group of linked computers between which data flow.

Neurology: the scientific study of the nervous system, especially its structure, functions, and abnormalities.

Neuron: an individual nerve cell that transmits electrical signals or impulses.

Neuroscience: the study of the nervous system and its components.

Neurotransmitter: a chemical that transmits electrical impulses (information) between nerve cells or nerve and muscle cells.

Neutron star: the extremely dense, compact, neutron-filled remains of a star that has exploded at the end of its lifetime.

Noncooperative games: games in which it is not possible for participants to form agreements with one another; each player is solely interested in his or her own gain.

Nonzero-sum game: a game in which the amount lost by all players is not equal to the amount won by all other players.

Nuclear fission: a nuclear reaction in which an atomic nucleus splits into two or more roughly equal, smaller nuclei, releasing huge amounts of energy in the process.

Nuclear fusion: a nuclear reaction in which two small atomic nuclei combine (fuse) with each other to form a larger nucleus, releasing huge amounts of energy in the process.

Nuclear magnetic resonance: application of radio waves to samples of certain elements in the presence of a strong magnetic field; this causes the nuclei to spin at a particular frequency and can be used to determine the structure of molecules. Its medical application is called magnetic resonance imaging.

Nuclear power: power generated by nuclear fission or nuclear fusion; the term typically refers to a controlled nuclear reaction from which energy is harnessed to produce electricity.

Nuclear reactor: facility where energy released by nuclear fission is harnessed and used to produce electricity; also called a nuclear power plant.

Nucleic acid: a complex organic compound stored in the cell nucleus that carries genetic information.

Nucleotide: the basic unit of a nucleic acid; it consists of a simple sugar, a phosphate group, and a nitrogen-containing base.

O

Orthogenesis: the theory that evolution is directed toward the development of more and more advanced species, culminating in humans.

Ozone: gas comprised of three atoms of oxygen. Ozone exists in a beneficial layer in the upper atmosphere that protects us from the Sun's harmful rays. Surface ozone is a layer of air pollution at Earth's surface formed by fossil fuel emissions and sunlight.

Ozone hole: region of very low ozone concentration above the Antarctic that appears and disappears with each austral (Southern Hemisphere) summer.

P

Paleontology: the scientific study of the life of past geological periods as known from fossil remains.

Patent: legal document granting an inventor exclusive rights to the production and marketing of his or her invention.

Pellagra: a disease caused by a deficiency of niacin and characterized by severe skin problems and diarrhea.

Penicillin: a chemical produced in common molds that has potent antibacterial properties; it is effective at treating a broad range of bacterial infections in humans.

Personal computer (PC): type of computer that sits on a desktop and is found in homes and schools; also called a microcomputer.

Pesticides: toxic chemicals used to kill insects, plants, or fungi that destroy crops.

Phenotype: the visible characteristics or physical shape produced by a living thing's genotype.

Photochemical smog: commonly called smog, it is a layer of air pollution at Earth's surface. The primary component of photochemical smog is surface ozone, an odorless, colorless gas comprised of three atoms of oxygen that is formed when polluting chemicals, such as those emitted by car exhaust systems, react with strong sunlight.

Photosynthesis: chemical process by which plants containing chlorophyll use sunlight to manufacture their own food by converting carbon dioxide and water to carbohydrates, releasing oxygen as a by-product.

Physiology: the branch of biology that deals with the functions and actions of life or of living matter, such as organs, tissues, and cells.

Plastics: lightweight, waterproof, and durable materials that can be shaped or molded with heat.

Plate: (or tectonic plate) large section of Earth's crust; also called tectonic plate.

Plate tectonics: the geologic theory that Earth's crust is made up of rigid plates that move about in response to internal pressure, creating the major geologic features on the planet's surface.

Polymer: complex molecule formed by chains of smaller, identical molecules.

Population: a complete set of individuals, objects, or events that belong to the same category.

Probability: the likelihood that something will happen.

Proteome: all the proteins in the human body.

Public health: the branch of medicine concerned with community-based efforts to prevent disease, promote health, and prolong life.

Pulsar: the rapidly spinning, blinking neutron-filled remains of a massive star that has exploded at the end of its lifetime.

Punctuated equilibrium: The theory that geologic change takes the form of periodic catastrophe as well as slow, steady accumulation of minuscule effects.

Q

Quasar: an extremely bright, starlike source of radio waves that is the oldest known type of object in the universe.

R

Radiation: the word comes from a Latin term that means "ray of light"; it is used in a general sense to cover all forms of energy that travel through space from one place to another as "rays."

Radio astronomy: the study of objects in space by observing the radio waves they create.

Radio interferometer: a system of multiple radio telescopes linked electronically that act as a single telescope with a diameter equal to the area separating them. Powerful computers combine their information and create detailed pictures of objects in space.

Radio waves: the longest form of electromagnetic radiation, some measuring up to 6 miles (9 kilometers) from peak to peak.

Radioactive decay: the predictable manner in which a population of atoms of a radioactive element spontaneously disintegrate over time.

Radioactive fallout: the radioactive particles resulting from a nuclear explosion.

Radioactive isotope: an isotope that spontaneously breaks down into another isotope with the release of some form of radiation.

Radioactivity: the property possessed by some elements of spontaneously emitting energy in the form of particles or waves by disintegration of their atomic nuclei.

Radiotherapy: the use of radiation to shrink cancerous tumors.

Range: the difference between the largest and smallest numbers in a set of observations.

Recessive trait: a trait that is expressed in offspring only when identical genes for the trait are inherited from both parents.

Recombinant DNA: a genetic engineering technique that involves the splicing of genes from two different organisms. This process results in hybrid DNA molecules with properties that are different from either of the parent organisms. Also called gene-splicing.

Resistant bacteria: strain of bacteria that previously would have been killed by a certain type of antibiotic but, over time, has become immune to that antibiotic's effect.

Rickets: a bone-weakening disease caused by a deficiency of vitamin D.

Rossby waves: long waves that are components of upper-air winds in the middle latitudes. At any given time, the entire hemisphere is encircled by just two to five Rossby waves.

S

Sample: some subset of a population that is representative of the entire population.

Scurvy: disease that results from a deficiency of vitamin C in which connective tissue in bone and muscle is weakened causing bleeding gums, bruising, and severe weakness.

Search engine: a computer program that scans a database of Web page addresses and picks out Web sites relevant to a given topic.

Semiconductor: nonmetallic solid element such as silicon or germanium that controls and strengthens an electric current. It acts like a conductor (facilitates the flow of electricity) in some situations and an insulator (blocks the flow of electricity) in others.

Sewage system: system of treating sewage (wastewater) to acceptable standards of cleanliness before discharging it to lakes or rivers.

Smog: common name for photochemical smog, a layer of hazy, brown air pollution at Earth's surface comprised of surface ozone.

Sociobiology: the science that deals with the social aspects of behavior as a product of evolution.

Software: computer programs and languages.

Solar eclipse: the complete or partial blocking of the Sun that occurs when the moon's orbit takes it between Earth and the Sun.

Space-time: a four-dimensional construct that unites the three dimensions of space (length, width, and height) and a fourth dimension, time.

Special creation: a worldview that embraces religious tenets, including divine creation from nothing, distinct kinds of plants and animals, a worldwide flood, and a relatively recent origin of the universe.

Special theory of relativity: German-born American physicist Einstein's theory—applicable to situations in which the rate of motion is constant—that space and time are not fixed, but change depending on how fast and in what direction the observer is moving.

Species: groups of living things that can breed together in the wild.

Speed of light: the speed at which light travels in a vacuum: 186,282.397 miles per second (299,274 kilometers per second).

Spinal cord: the part of the central nervous system extending from the brain along the back in the cavity of the spinal column.

Standard deviation: the square root of the variance; this measure is useful for determining how far, and in what numbers, measurements in a sample are spread from the mean.

Steam engine: an engine that converts steam to mechanical energy.

Subduction: the process that occurs when two tectonic plates come together; the edge of one plate slides beneath the other and undergoes partial melting.

Submersible: a ship capable of operating at great depths in the ocean.

Sulfa drugs: also called sulfanilamides; the first chemicals used to treat bacterial infections; they are distilled from dyes that bind tightly to wool.

Supernova: an explosion of a massive star at the end of its lifetime, causing it to shine more brightly than the rest of the stars in the galaxy.

Sustainable agriculture: system of farming that emphasizes environmental protection and soil maintenance as well as high yields.

Symbiotic: describes a relationship in which two or more organisms live in close connection with each other, often to the benefit of both or all organisms.

Synapse: the junction between nerve cells in the brain through which neurotransmitters travel and where the exchange of electrical or chemical information takes place.

Synthetic: any material that is produced in a laboratory from synthetic (nonliving) materials.

T

Taxonomy: the laws and principles of classifying living things.

Transistor: tiny electronic component consisting of three layers of semiconductor material that amplifies and controls electric currents.

Tumor: a swollen part or growth.

Turbine: a shaft with a circle of blades that turns and generates power.

Turbocompressor: turbine-driven air compressor, such as that in a jet engine.

U

Ultrasound: a technique that uses high-frequency sound waves beyond the frequency range that humans can hear to see inside the body; also called ultrasonics or ultrasonography.

V

Vaccination: the process of injecting weakened or dead disease-causing bacteria or viruses into a person, to create immunity (protection from infection) to a specific disease; also called inoculation or immunization.

Vacuum tube: early electronic device that looks like a lightbulb; similar to a transistor, it controls the direction and strength of an electric current.

Vitamins: organic substances found mainly in foods that are essential in minute quantities for growth and health.

Volcano: an opening, or vent, in Earth's surface through which lava, rock fragments, ash, and gas escape.

W

Warm front: the line behind which a warm air mass is advancing and in front of which a cold air mass is retreating.

Water energy: energy contained in flowing rivers, the rise and fall of the tides, and ocean waves.

Water wheel: a simple device used to harness water energy consisting of a series of paddles that rotate around a central shaft.

Web browser: software that allows the user to access the World Wide Web and the Internet and to read and search for information.

World Wide Web: the Internet's primary service for accessing information.

X

X ray: a form of electromagnetic radiation with a wavelength about 1,000 times shorter than visible light.

Z

Zero-sum game: a game in which the amount lost by all players is equal to the amount won by all other players.

Zygote: a fertilized egg.

chapter two Mathematics

1900 German mathematician David Hilbert makes a historic address to the International Congress of Mathematicians in Paris, in which he poses a set of twenty-three problems for mathematicians to solve in the twentieth century.

1907 Emmy Amalie Noether, one of the first women allowed to attend classes at a German university, earns her Ph.D. in mathematics and graduates at the top of her class.

1925 British statistician and geneticist Sir Ronald Aylmer Fisher publishes the landmark textbook *Statistical Methods for Research Workers*.

1933 The Nazi government in Germany passes the Law for the Restoration of the Professional Civil Service, ordering the removal of Jews and their supporters from state employment—including universities.

1936 British mathematician Alan M. Turing writes "On Computable Numbers," in which he describes a theoretical computer that provides a blueprint for the modern digital computer.

1940 The American Mathematical Society founds *Mathematical Reviews*, a journal that stands at the center of international mathematical publishing for the rest of the century.

1944 Hungarian-American mathematician John von Neumann and German-American economist Oskar Morgenstern apply game theory to economic competition in their classic book *Theory of Games and Economic Behavior*.

1946 The first electronic computer in the United States, the ENIAC (Electronic Numerical Integrator and Computer), is completed.

1949 Evelyn Boyd Granville is awarded her doctorate by Yale University, becoming the first African American woman to earn a Ph.D. in mathematics.

1960s New Math, a method of teaching mathematics to children that stresses conceptual (or intuitive) understanding of the foundations of mathematics, is launched.

1971 American mathematicians Alice T. Schafer and Mary Gray found the Association for Women in Mathematics (AWM), a nonprofit organization that supports women in the mathematical sciences.

1989 A "newer" New Math, usually called standards math, is developed and put into practice in more than 40 states; it emphasizes teamwork, the use of three-dimensional objects, and problem solving in real-life situations.

1993 British mathematician Andrew Wiles offers a proof for history's most famous unsolved mathematical problem: Fermat's last theorem.

1994 American mathematician John Forbes Nash wins a Nobel Prize in economics for his work on noncooperative game theory.

Background

Mathematics in the twentieth century continued to explore patterns and relationships (of shapes, numbers, and changes in quantity, for instance). Such exploration is necessary to examine and describe the physical world, as well as to solve scientific problems. Branches of mathematics developed in the twentieth century, such as game theory and statistics, have had many real-world applications—among them the development and assessment of military, economic, and political strategy. In addition, the capabilities of mathematicians in the twentieth century were greatly expanded by the development of computers.

Just as important as *what* mathematicians were pursuing in the twentieth century were *who* was involved in mathematical scholarship and *how* math was being presented to students. One significant development was the shift of the international center of mathematics from Germany to the United States during World War II (1939–45). Another trend in both Europe and the United States was the increasing number of women in the mathematics community. And in the United States, African Americans took advantage of new opportunities to become important mathematicians. In the latter half of the century, efforts at improving the math abilities of American students gave rise to new teaching methods such as New Math and standards math, as well as a serious debate over how to make math seem important to young people.

Computational mathematics

Since World War II, computers have revolutionized mathematics, scientific inquiry, and engineering design. Computers proved capable of solving difficult problems that had been impossible to figure out in the past. Supercomputers, which analyze huge amounts of data, became vital in weather forecasting, as well as in the modeling of nuclear explosions, airflow around airplane wings, and other physical phenomena. Computers have also enhanced mathematical inquiry by carrying out massive operations at lightning-quick speeds, thereby freeing mathematicians from the grunt work of endless calculations.

One example of a computer-assisted discovery is fractals, mathematical objects defined as curves or surfaces generated by continual subdivision. The discovery of fractals has had a significant impact on several fields, including physical chemistry and physiology. Computational mathematics has also led to the design of improved technologies and has been key to gaining a more complete understanding of the universe.

Game theory

Another mathematical tool that saw its greatest development in the twentieth century is game theory, the branch of mathematics that analyzes conflict situations. Game theory offers insights into the strategic choices made by individuals and groups (such as governments, corporations, and armies). Mathematicians use game theory to evaluate the costs and benefits of certain strategies in military and business decisions, political campaigns, jury selection, investment decisions, medical analysis, and political lobbying. They also use it to study aggression, cooperation, and hunting methods in animals.

Game theory has seen its greatest applications in economic and military decisions. Corporations and government regulatory agencies use it to study behaviors such as consumer spending, competition, and price-fixing. Businesses rely on game theory when figuring out how much profit they can expect to make from a product and where to locate a new manufacturing plant or store. In addition, both the United States and the Soviet Union used game theory during the Cold War (an economic and military standoff between the two countries that lasted from 1945 to 1990) to develop military policy. Out of game theory came the controversial idea of mutual assured destruction: that if the Soviet Union and the United States both had a large number of nuclear weapons, neither nation would use them because it would result in the destruction of both countries.

Statistics

Statistics is the branch of mathematics concerned with collecting, interpreting, and presenting numerical data. In the nineteenth century, statisticians focused on collecting huge amounts of data. In the twentieth century, the field grew to include analyzing, explaining, and drawing conclusions about the data, as well as developing tools to make sure those conclusions were accurate and reliable.

Currently every branch of experimental science uses statistics, not to mention industry, entertainment, government, and sports. For instance, statistics can paint a picture of the nation's ethnic and racial diversity, employment and unemployment, worker productivity, sports league standings, CD sales, and rainfall. Statistics in the twentieth century offered a means of measuring and learning about almost every aspect of the natural and physical world.

International mathematical center shifts to United States

Before the 1930s, the world's center of mathematics was Germany. Germany had earned this status in the 1600s and 1700s, during the period of political and scientific inquiry known as the Enlightenment. Many of the scientists and mathematicians drawn to German universities at that time were of Jewish ancestry. Germany became home to the world's two mathematics journals of record, and German became the main language of international mathematical discussion.

This ended in 1933 with the rise to power of Adolf Hitler (1889–1945), the leader of the National Socialist (Nazi) Party. One of the first steps in the Nazis' program of discriminating against and persecuting Jews was to fire Jewish faculty members from German universities. As a result, many German intellectuals left the country; the largest concentration of them ended up in the United States. As a result of this "brain drain" from Germany— which included such notable scientists and mathematicians as Albert Einstein (1879–1955), Hans Bethe (1906–), Hermann Weyl (1885–1955), Olga Taussky-Todd (1906–1995), and Emmy Noether (1882–1935)—the new center of the mathematical world shifted to the United States.

Women in mathematics

Another distinguishing characteristic of mathematics in the 1900s was the emergence of women in the field. In earlier times, women had been effectively barred from the field by being kept out of universities and mathematical societies. In the late nineteenth and early twentieth centuries, however, learning institutions began to change their rules, and women enrolled in undergraduate and graduate programs in mathematics.

The first woman to officially earn a Ph.D. in mathematics (at the German University of Göttengin in 1896) was the Englishwoman Grace Emily Chisholm Young (1868–1944). The most famous were Emmy Noether of Germany; Olga Taussky-Todd of Austria; and Americans Anna Pell Wheeler (1883–1966), Olive Clio Hazlett (1890–1974), and Julia Bowman Robinson (1919–1985). Despite the accomplishments of female mathematicians, at the end of the twentieth century women were still seriously underrepresented on the mathematics faculties of major universities.

African Americans in mathematics

Another group of individuals who entered mathematics in the twentieth century were African Americans. Due to segregation (separation of the races) laws, Americans of African heritage were denied entrance to many colleges and universities until the mid-1960s.

The first African American to earn a Ph.D. in mathematics was Elbert F. Cox (1895–1969), at Cornell University in 1925. The most respected twentieth-century African American mathematician, who specialized in theoretical statistics and game theory, was David Blackwell (1919–). Blackwell earned his Ph.D. at the University of Illinois in 1941. Several female African American mathematicians also emerged during the twentieth century, most notably Evelyn Boyd Granville (1924–), who in 1949 became the first African American woman to receive a Ph.D. in mathematics; Marjorie Lee Browne (1914–1979); and Etta Z. Falconer (1933–).

By the year 2000, while some 300 African Americans had earned advanced degrees in mathematics, concerns persisted that African Americans were almost nonexistent among tenured mathematics faculty at major universities. The end of the century also saw a growing concern over the poor overall performance of African American youth in mathematics, as well as the birth of various organizations and programs aimed at improving the math skills of young African Americans.

New Math

Throughout much of the twentieth century, the United States trailed other industrialized nations in its children's math skills. In an era marked by technological advances, this has at times been raised to the status of a national crisis. Many people have suggested solutions, and some of those have been put into practice, but none has met with unqualified success or gained widespread support from educators and parents.

In the 1960s experts in mathematical education developed a program called New Math. This strategy downplayed the traditional method of memorizing math facts and formulas in favor of teaching a conceptual, or intuitive, understanding of the foundations of mathematics. New Math was judged a failure within a decade, mostly because of the confusion it caused in teachers and parents. The era of New Math was followed by a return to traditional math education.

In 1989, with no improvement seen in American students' math test scores, the National Council of Teachers of Mathematics (NCTM) proposed a new set of math standards. This new program included some elements of New Math while stressing cooperation, teamwork, and real-life problem solving. Called "the new New Math" and "Fuzzy Math" by its opponents, standards math (so-named because it follows NCTM standards) remained a controversial teaching approach at the close of the twentieth century.

☐ THE DEVASTATION OF MATHEMATICS IN HITLER'S GERMANY

Overview

In 1933, when Adolf Hitler (1889–1945) came to power in Germany, his National Socialist (Nazi) Party began its campaign of persecution against the Jewish people. One of the earliest steps in the process that ended in the murder of millions of Jews during World War II (1939–45), known as the Holocaust, was firing Jewish professors and lecturers (mainly in science and math departments) from German universities. This action resulted in a "brain drain" as some of Germany's best minds left for friendlier shores—mainly in North America. As a result, the center of the mathematical world moved from Germany to the United States and Canada.

Background

From the thirteenth century through the present, Jewish people in Europe have faced discrimination of varying intensity. In the 1600s and 1700s Europe experienced the Enlightenment, a period of free political and scientific inquiry and a belief in the power of human reason (as opposed to superstition and religion). Jews and other members of ethnic and religious minorities enjoyed greater professional and economic opportunities than they had previously. At the same time, Germany's relatively large Jewish population—a subgroup that valued scholarship and scientific reasoning—was interested in interacting more with the population at large.

One of the Enlightenment's most notable advances, particularly in Germany, was a blossoming of science and mathematics. Literature and art, which had been taught in universities for a long time, had relatively few minority faculty members. Math and science, in contrast, were new fields that accepted a diverse group of teachers. Many Jewish scholars took advantage of this relatively tolerant atmosphere to establish university careers.

In the 1870s, Germany faced an economic depression. As in other difficult periods, Jews were made scapegoats and faced increased repression. Anti-Semitism (discrimination against Jews) increased and decreased for the next fifty years, but it rose steeply in the 1920s following Germany's defeat in World War I (1914–18) and the economic depression that followed. Hitler, when he became leader of the nation, tapped into the anti-Jewish sentiment and raised it to new heights.

Hitler's rise creates chilly academic climate

When Hitler took power in January 1933, few intellectuals believed that his fascist politics would affect German universities. (Fascism is a political system characterized by a dictator with complete power, the forcible suppression of opposition, and the promotion of nationalism and racism.) Within months, however, they were proved wrong.

Even before legal measures were put in place, hostility toward Jews began to rise in academic circles. The increase in anti-Semitism gave rise to individuals like Ludwig Bieberbach (1886–1982), a mathematics professor who denounced Jewish professors for teaching what he called "alien mathematics." Student supporters of Hitler also tried to intimidate Jewish students and professors by dressing in brown shirts, similar to the uniforms worn by Hitler's storm troopers, members of a paramilitary group known for its violence against Jews and political opponents.

Purge of Jewish professors

In April 1933 Hitler's government passed the Law for the Restoration of the Professional Civil Service, which ordered that Jews and their supporters be removed from state employment. Since German universities were run by the state, the law applied to university instructors. At first Jews who had served in the German army during World War I were not forced out, but many professors who were spared for that reason resigned to protest the

Adolf Hitler and his soldiers.

Edmund Georg Landau

One of the highest-profile German mathematicians who was persecuted by the Nazis was Edmund Georg Hermann Landau (1877–1938). Born in Berlin to a Jewish father, Landau was trained in mathematics at Berlin University, where he earned his Ph.D. in 1899 for a dissertation on number theory (the study of the arithmetical properties of whole numbers and methods of writing numbers).

Landau began teaching at Berlin University in 1901. He was a popular instructor and respected researcher. In 1903 Landau rose to international fame when he simplified the proof of Gauss's prime-number theorem. (German mathematician Karl Friedrich Gauss [1777–1855] had developed a theorem regarding the density of prime numbers; his mathematical formula determined how many prime numbers exist in a given range of numbers.) In 1910 Landau accepted a position as professor of mathematics at the University of Göttingen. He remained there for the rest of his career, teaching and publishing several books on number theory.

In 1933, about one year after Hitler's rise to power, Landau was forced out of his position at the university. When Landau attempted to defy the order and continue teaching, he was blocked by troops of the SS (Hitler's elite guard). Although his career had been abruptly ended, Landau, who was near retirement age, made no attempt to flee Germany. He died of natural causes in Berlin in 1938.

treatment of their colleagues. In any case, that clause was removed in 1935 and all remaining Jews were fired from their university jobs.

In all, nearly 200 mathematicians had to leave their positions in Germany and Austria (Hitler's army took over Austria in 1938). Hundreds of other mathematicians from other parts of Europe, starting with Czechoslovakia in 1939, fled as Hitler's army began to advance on their countries.

While many mathematicians in the early 1930s accepted invitations to teach in the United States, Canada, and Great Britain, the worldwide economic depression in the 1930s generated widespread unemployment and poverty. Under those conditions, some nations were reluctant to admit refugees—even intellectuals. Some well-known professors were imprisoned (and in some cases killed) by Hitler's army or were forced to live as illegal aliens, working at low-level jobs or living off charity. Many of them lost what should have been the most productive years of their professional lives.

Impact

About seventy-five mathematicians who were forced to leave German universities made their new homes in the United States. Mathematicians from other parts of Europe also came to the United States and Canada. Among the most famous mathematicians and physicists to emigrate to the United States during the Nazi era were Albert Einstein (1879–1955), Hans Bethe (1906–), **Hermann Weyl** (1885–1955; see biography in this chapter), **Olga Taussky-Todd** (1906–1995; see biography in this chapter), and **Emmy Amalie Noether** (1882–1935; see biography in this chapter). As a result North America became the new international center of high-level mathematics research, and the refugee professors helped train a new generation of American mathematicians.

Mathematical Reviews *becomes journal of record*

Another effect of the purge of mathematicians from Germany during Hitler's rule was the transfer of the international mathematical journal of record from Germany to the United States. Prior to Hitler's rise to power, the world's two main mathematical journals, *Jahrbuch über die Fortschritte der Mathematik* and *Zentralblatt für Mathematik und ihre Grenzgebiete*, were both published in Germany. German was the main language for international mathematical discussions, and Germans controlled the process of peer-reviewing mathematical journal articles. (Peer-reviewing is the act of judging and criticizing articles submitted to professional journals; peer reviewers are people at the top of their fields.)

The downfall of the *Jahrbuch* began in 1933, when Ludwig Bieberbach, who was one of its editors, fired all the Jewish peer reviewers. Three years later the journal stopped covering mathematical physics, which was considered a Jewish discipline. *Zentralblatt* saw a similar decline. In the mid-1930s the journal's editor, Otto Neugebauer (1899–1990), fled to Denmark, and in 1938 his co-editor Tullio Levi-Civita (1873–1941), an Italian Jew, was fired. The publisher of the journal then barred Jews from reviewing papers written by German mathematicians.

In the 1920s mathematicians in the United States and Great Britain had tried unsuccessfully to establish mathematical journals similar to those produced in Germany. By the end of the 1930s, however, most of the

German journals' peer reviewers were living in North America, shifting the balance of power. In 1940 the American Mathematical Society founded *Mathematical Reviews* with Neugebauer as its head editor. The journal has remained at the center of mathematical publishing ever since.

Germany has yet to recover

In August 1998 the International Congress of Mathematicians (ICM) met in Germany for the first time since 1904. The event, held in Berlin, paid tribute to the fifty mathematicians from that city who were expelled and the three who were killed by Hitler's forces. The few surviving mathematicians who were victims of the Nazi era gave speeches as honored guests. German attendees at the ICM meeting expressed their hope that someday mathematics in their country would regain its former glory.

☐ THE DEVELOPMENT OF COMPUTATIONAL MATHEMATICS

Overview

Computers were first used after World War II (1939–45) to find the answers to complex problems in math, physics, and other scientific fields. Since that time computers have found solutions to increasingly difficult equations that were unsolvable in the past. Supercomputers (extremely fast and powerful computers) tackle problems that involve large amounts of data and complicated instructions, such as modeling weather systems, nuclear explosions, and airflow around airplane wings. The use of computers has revolutionized the fields of mathematics, scientific inquiry, and engineering design and made possible a number of new discoveries.

Background

The modern computer evolved from a long line of calculating machines that has its roots in ancient times. One of the earliest mechanical mathematical tools, developed in Asia more than 2,000 years ago, was the abacus, a device that makes calculations by moving stones or beads.

In the seventeenth century, a series of slide rules, each more sophisticated than the last, were invented to carry out multiplication, division, and other mathematical functions. The seventeenth century also saw the first mechanical calculators, desktop machines that were large, heavy, slow, and difficult to use. In 1645 French mathematician and physicist Blaise Pascal (1623–1662) created the pascaline, a series of eight joined rotary dials, each representing a different place of ten (i.e., 1, 10, 100, and so on), with notches on each dial for the numbers 0 through 9. Numbers up to nine digits long could be added or subtracted by turning each dial forward or backward the appropriate number of notches.

Thirty years later, German mathematician Gottfried Wilhelm Leibniz (1646–1716) created the Liebniz calculator, a turning-dial machine similar to the pascaline. Liebniz's invention was an improvement over previous machines in that it could multiply and divide as well as add and subtract.

Advent of computers

Mathematical-assistance devices took a huge leap in the twentieth century with the introduction of computers. Computers are different from calculators in that while a calculator contains one fixed set of instructions that tell it how to perform specific mathematical functions, the computer can be programmed and reprogrammed to perform an endless list of functions.

Many of the basic principles that guide modern computers were worked out by English astronomer and inventor Charles Babbage (1791–1871) in the 1820s. Babbage attempted to construct what would have been the first computer, which he called an "analytical engine," an enormous, steam-driven machine with thousands of gear wheels. In theory, his computer would be able to perform any kind of arithmetic and store the information on punched tape (a roll of paper on which information is encoded as a pattern of punched holes). As it turned out, the technology needed to complete such a machine would not exist for another 100 years.

World War II pushes need for technology

Military necessity forced the development of computers during World War II. British scientists, in the early 1940s, produced the first computer—the Colossus—to figure out German military codes. The earliest Colossus computers were driven by electric motors and contained a complex array

Mark I, the first general-purpose digital computer. (Courtesy of the Library of Congress.)

of shafts and gears. In 1943, the first electronic version of the Colossus was created. It was an enormous machine, containing 1,500 vacuum tubes (early electronic devices that control the direction and strength of an electrical current).

At the same time mathematicians and scientists in the American military were trying to produce a machine that would help solve ballistics (the motion of projectiles) problems for artillery shells. The result was that in 1944, the Mark I—the first programmable American computer to produce accurate results—was constructed at Harvard University. Essentially seventy-eight adding machines and calculators linked together, the Mark I could add or subtract numbers up to twenty-three digits long at a rate of three calculations per second and could perform some logic functions (based on a method of reasoning that figures out the logical consequences of a set of statements). Computer developments in England and the United States were key to their victory over Germany, Italy, and Japan in World War II.

Rapid improvement of electronic computers

Rapid advances in computer technology began after World War II and continued through the end of the century. The first electronic computer in the United States, called the ENIAC (Electronic Numerical Integrator and Computer), was completed in 1946. It could perform 5,000 addition or subtraction calculations per second and could also multiply, divide, figure square roots, and perform advanced logic functions. The ENIAC was followed in 1951 by the UNIVAC (Universal Automatic Computer), the first commercially available computer. Like the ENIAC, the UNIVAC was a huge computer that relied on thousands of heat-generating vacuum tubes.

In the next wave of computers, transistors replaced vacuum tubes. Invented in 1947, the transistor is a solid-state electronic component (meaning it has no heated wires or moving parts) made of semiconductor material—such as germanium or silicon—that can control or strengthen an electrical current. Transistors are superior to vacuum tubes in many ways: they are much smaller, generate almost no heat, are more reliable, and consume far less energy. With transistors, computers became much more practical to build, maintain, and operate. Since the early 1960s, manufacturers have been using integrated circuits (thumbnail-sized pieces of semiconductor material, usually silicon, that each hold millions of transistors and other electronic components) to construct ever-smaller computers with increased power, speed, and memory storage.

Impact

The development of sophisticated computers has made it possible to complete complex mathematical calculations and solve problems that were considered unsolvable before. Computers are also valuable in that they carry out massive operations at lightning-quick speeds and free up mathematicians from the drudgery of making these calculations themselves. Mathematicians also use computers to make new discoveries, for instance, they can instruct a computer to repeat a mathematical operation a million times and then analyze the results. Such a process led to the discovery of fractals, shapes that maintain similar properties and relationships at all levels of magnification. Each component part of the fractal, when magnified, resembles the structure as a whole. Fractal concepts have seen widespread application in areas such as astronomy (particularly in studying how galaxies form), cellular processes, and computer animation.

The use of computers in mathematics has made possible the design of better machines and has led to a more complete understanding of our universe. It is reasonable to predict that with the continuing development of better and faster computers, computational mathematics will be even more significant in the future.

Austrian physicist Erwin Schrödinger was the first to study wave mechanics. (Courtesy of the Library of Congress.)

Computers answer previously unsolvable problems

The first purely scientific problem that electronic computers took on in the 1950s and 1960s was the wave equation of Austrian physicist Erwin Schrödinger (1887–1961). The wave equation, one of the central equations in the field of quantum mechanics (the physical principles used to explain submicroscopic phenomena), describes the "probability waves" that determine the motion of electrons (small particles found in atoms). Although written in the late 1920s, the wave equation was so complex that it could not be proved (although theoretical predictions agreed with the results of experiments). It was not until the 1990s that supercomputers provided satisfactory numerical answers to the wave equation, giving us a better understanding of how atoms are structured.

Computers analyze tremendous data sets

Another area in which computers are instrumental is weather forecasting. The National Weather Service's supercomputer, known as Cray YMP/832, can perform 2 billion computations each second—a task that if done by hand would require the efforts of 123,000 people. The supercomputer is programmed with series of mathematical equations called computer models. These models use laws of mathematics and fluid dynamics to create scenarios that imitate what occurs in the atmosphere under given sets of conditions. (Computer models are also useful for making climate projections, such as predicting how the gradual warming of the Earth will affect conditions fifty or one hundred years from now.)

The weather supercomputer analyzes data and churns out 20,000 forecasts and 6,000 weather maps each day. Before the mid-1950s, when weather forecasters began using computers, they could only predict the weather thirty-six hours in advance. Today, they can make daily forecasts six to ten days in advance.

☐ THE DEVELOPMENT OF GAME THEORY

Overview
Game theory is the branch of mathematics concerned with the analysis of conflict situations. It makes predictions about the behavior of competitors that are operating with a mixture of interests and goals and offers insights into how individuals and groups (such as governments, corporations, and armies) make strategic choices and maximize their advantages. By using game theory, a person can choose the best strategy to use in a given situation and the costs and benefits associated with that strategy. Game theory has been used in military and business endeavors, political campaigns, jury selection, investment decisions, medical analysis, political lobbying, and more. Recent studies analyzing various aspects of animal behavior, such as aggression, cooperation, and hunting, have used game theory as well.

Background
Game theory got its start in the seventeenth century by mathematicians attempting to develop strategies for winning at poker and other card games. French mathematicians Blaise Pascal (1623–1662) and Pierre de Fermat (1601–1665), at the request of a gentleman gambler, figured out how to predict the likelihood of drawing certain hands (for example, a flush, a straight, or three of a kind) in poker. The next mathematician to advance game theory was the Frenchman **Félix-Édouard-Justin-Émile Borel** (1871–1956; see biography in this chapter), who wrote a series of papers on the mathematical foundation of strategies that combined rational choices with chance.

Hungarian-born American mathematician John von Neumann (1903– 1957; see box on pages 130-131) applied game theory to a range of other disciplines. In 1928 Von Neumann, who became aware of game

John von Neumann

John von Neumann.
(Reproduced by permission of
the Corbis Corporation.)

Hungarian-born American mathemati-cian John von Neumann (1903–1957) is credited with writing the first computer pro-gram (a long sequence of instructions that tells the computer how to process informa-tion), establishing random access-memory (RAM), and developing the use of input and output devices (e.g., keyboards and printers) for computers. He proved that a computer can carry out any computation, no matter how complex, by following a series of simple steps. Von Neumann is also noted for his devel-opment of game theory (a method of using games to simulate complex decision-making processes) and quantum mechanics (physical principles used to describe submicroscopic phenomena).

Von Neumann earned his Ph.D. in mathematics at the University of Budapest in Hungary in 1926; three years later he emigrated to the United States and joined the faculty of Princeton University. In 1933 he accepted a position at Princeton's Institute for Advanced Study (IAS). During World War II (1939–45), von Neumann joined the Manhattan Project, the U.S. government's secret program to design and construct the world's first atomic weapon.

theory through Borel's work, established the minimax theorem as a solu-tion for certain games. Von Neumann's greatest contribution to the field, however, was demonstrating that games like poker, chess, or betting on a coin toss could provide profound insights into complex economic and

In the mid-1940s von Neumann became interested in ENIAC (Electronic Numerical Integrator and Computer), the world's first electronic computer. Developed for use by the U.S. Army, the massive computer's greatest drawback was that it was not programmable; it could only be set up to solve a particular problem by physically arranging electrical circuits. Von Neumann became a consultant to engineers working on an improved computer, which was named EDVAC (Electronic Discrete Variable Automatic Computer).

In June 1945 von Neumann published his design for a programmable computer in a paper titled "First Draft of a Report on EDVAC." He argued that computers were capable of performing a wide range of functions, and even of taking the results of their computations and using them to solve new equations. He compared the electrical circuits of a computer to the neurons of a brain. The EDVAC was built using von Neumann's program design and thus became the first computer with a stored program.

In the latter half of the 1940s, Von Neumann constructed his own computer. Housed at the IAS and funded by the U.S. government, Von Neumann's machine, known as the IAS computer, was completed in 1951. The computer contained the following basic elements, in separate compartments, that are still found in computers today: a program; input and output components; memory; and a central unit for processing mathematics, logic, and control functions. It performed functions faster than any other computer of that era.

During his final years, von Neumann served on the Atomic Energy Commission. He was diagnosed with bone cancer in 1955 and confined to a wheelchair, but he continued to work until his death in 1957.

social problems. Von Neumann pointed out that the value of game theory is rooted in three elements: game playing is a universal experience, games incorporate strategy, and gaming experiments can be easily tested with human subjects.

cooperative game: a game in which players join together to achieve the maximum total payoff for the group.

game: a situation in which a conflict arises between two or more players.

game theory: the branch of mathematics concerned with analyzing conflict situations; it provides a model for understanding and predicting the behavior of competitors in situations where the participants are driven by varying interests and goals.

games of incomplete information: games such as poker, in which players make decisions without full knowledge about the various elements of the game.

minimax theorem: the central theorem of game theory. It states that for any two-player zero-sum game, there is a strategy that leads to a solution in which both players guarantee their maximum payoff and one player's expected gain will exactly equal the other's expected loss.

Nash equilibrium: a solution for noncooperative games, proposed by John Forbes Nash (1928–), that provides a way for all players' expectations to be met and strategies optimized.

noncooperative game: a game in which participants cannot form agreements with one another; each player is solely interested in his or her own gain.

nonzero-sum game: a game in which the amount lost by all players is not equal to the amount won by all other players.

zero-sum game: a game in which the amount lost by all players is equal to the amount won by all other players.

Game theory attracted little interest until von Neumann teamed up with German-born American economist Oskar Morgenstern (1902–1977) in 1944 and applied game theory to economic competition in the classic book *Theory of Games and Economic Behavior.* That book laid the foundation for all subsequent work in game theory. Many economists, mathematicians (including John Forbes Nash; see box on pages 134-135), and others have since contributed to the development and application of game theory.

What is a game?

A game, which may be as simple as tic-tac-toe or as complex as a military battle, must feature a conflict between two or more participants in which some parties gain and other parties lose. A game must start with certain predetermined conditions, such as the way cards are dealt or the way soldiers are positioned on a battlefield. Throughout the game, there must be defined choices, made either by the players themselves or by a random device, such as a roll of the dice. The game must end after a set number of moves, at which time a winner is declared. The outcome of the game indicates what payments (positive, negative, or zero) each player will receive.

Categories of games

Games fall into certain categories, based on the type of information available to players when they make their choices. In a "game of perfect information," such as chess or checkers, there is no hidden information. Each player has full knowledge of every move made previously during the game, and each player has access to the same information. Another factor that defines this type of game is that there is one best strategy for each player that provides the best outcome, regardless of the strategy used by his or her opponent.

In a "game of imperfect information," such as poker, each participant has access to different information, and none of the participants has access to all of the information. A poker player only knows which cards are in his or her own hand, not which cards are in the other players' hands or which cards have not been dealt. In these types of games, no one strategy guarantees the best outcome. A player can only apply a "probabilistic strategy" to find the solution to the game. In other words, players must make guesses based on how likely it is that certain events will occur.

Two-player zero-sum games

The simplest games, and the type to which game theory strategies are most often and most easily applied, are called two-player zero-sum games. In those games, there are two competing parties, and the amount gained by the winner is equal to the amount lost by the loser. An example of this type of game is matching pennies. In that game, each player places a penny on a table, keeping their hands over their coins. Then they remove their hands and reveal whether the side facing up is heads or tails. If the same face is showing on both coins—two heads or two tails—player A wins. If one penny is heads and the other is tails, player B wins. When A wins a penny, B loses a penny, and vice versa.

John Nash.
(Reproduced by permission of
Mr. John F. Nash, Jr.)

American mathematician John Forbes Nash (1928–) is a pioneer in the field of game theory. In 1950, at the age of twenty-two, he earned his Ph.D. in mathematics from Princeton University for a dissertation on noncooperative games (games in which participants cannot form agreements with one another; each player is solely interested in his or her own gain). Nash created the theory of equilibrium in noncooperative games—also called the Nash equilibrium—which determined how to predict the exchange of needs, wants, and threats among competitors. The Nash equilibrium also offered a solution for noncooperative games in which all players' expectations could be met and their strategies optimized.

In the above example, there is no move for either player that will guarantee a win. If one player were to have advance knowledge of which face would show on his or her opponent's coin, however, that player could choose a strategy in order to win. For instance, if A knew that B played heads every time, A would also play heads.

The minimax theorem

The central theorem of game theory, which applies to situations such as the matching pennies game, is called the minimax theorem. Developed by John von Neumann, this theory states that for any two-player zero-sum game there is a strategy (known as an "optimal probabilistic strategy") that leads to a solution guaranteeing each player their maximum payoff. In the matching pennies game, the minimax theorem would advise each

Noncooperative game theory is widely considered one of the most important developments in twentieth-century mathematics, economics, and social science. For his work on noncooperative game theory, Nash won a Nobel Prize in economics in 1994.

Nash was a professor at the Massachusetts Institute of Technology (MIT) for a short time after earning his Ph.D. but was forced to resign for health reasons. For three decades, Nash was beset by paranoid schizophrenia, a mental illness marked by bizarre and delusional behavior, and was hospitalized several times. When he could, he worked as a mathematics consultant at a variety of policy institutes. Nash also frequently visited the MIT campus, where he would leave mathematical notations and writings scrawled on empty classroom blackboards in the mathematics building.

In the early 1990s Nash made a sudden recovery from his illness. Since that time he has continued to work on game theory and other mathematical pursuits. The 2001 Academy-Award-winning film *A Beautiful Mind,* starring Russell Crowe, was based on the life of John Nash.

player to randomly select heads or tails 50 percent of the time; the expected gain (or loss) for both players would be zero. Because of this expected outcome, in which both players end up no better off than when they started, the minimax theorem concludes that for many two-person zero-sum games, there is no point in playing.

Nonzero-sum games

The majority of conflict situations, however, are nonzero-sum games that involve more than two parties. The amount gained by the winners, in such cases, is not equal to the amount given up by the losers. While the minimax theorem does not apply to these games, various other solutions—cooperative and noncooperative—can be used.

A "cooperative solution" requires two or more parties to form a coalition, a group that behaves as a single player. The purpose of forming a coalition is to achieve the maximum possible payoff for the group. In a "noncooperative solution," each player acts solely in his or her own interest and does not form alliances. The purpose of behaving in a noncooperative manner is to maximize the payoff for oneself. While the potential gain is greatest in the noncooperative solution, so is the potential loss.

Impact

Game theory has proved useful for selecting the best strategy or outcome in situations ranging from economic decisions to military campaigns. Supporters of game theory believe that it can apply to a broad range of both simple and complex situations. Its critics argue that game theory only applies to a few selected scenarios in which there are a limited number of competitors. Some economists claim that game theory cannot accurately predict outcomes in an arena as complex as free economic competition.

Game theory and military strategy

Game theory was widely used during the Cold War (an economic and military standoff between the United States and the Soviet Union that lasted from 1945 to 1990) to analyze specific military operations, as well as for general policies such as those governing nuclear weapons. Game theory is credited with helping to shape the policy of "mutual assured destruction," the idea that if the Soviet Union and the United States both had a large number of nuclear weapons, neither nation would use them because it would result in the destruction of both countries.

Not everyone approves of the use of game theory to analyze military strategies. Critics charge that game theory only considers battles in terms of victories or defeats without taking into account the human cost of the strategy. They argue that such an attitude is dangerous because it ignores human suffering.

Other applications of game theory

Another field that frequently uses game theory is economics. Government agencies that regulate industry use game theory to create antitrust laws (laws that prevent large corporations from gaining control of a given industry and promote competition). Companies use it to decide how to price new products, where to locate a new store or factory, and whether to buy other businesses.

Game theory has also proved useful in the field of public health, particularly in organizing immunization campaigns to protect people from disease and testing new medicines. Political strategists employ it to plan electoral campaigns and lobbying efforts. Attorneys have used game theory to decide when to exercise their right to dismiss possible jurors.

☐ ADVANCES IN THE FIELD OF STATISTICS

Overview
Statistics is the branch of mathematics concerned with collecting, presenting, and interpreting numerical data. It provides a theoretical framework for analyzing and explaining trends in and drawing conclusions from collected information. The field of statistics provides ways of measuring and learning about almost every aspect of the world around us.

There are two major divisions of statistics: descriptive statistics and inferential statistics. The former deals with the simple collection, presentation, and interpretation of numerical data. The latter focuses on predictions and trends; it analyzes data from a sample (a subset of a population; in statistics, a population is a complete set of individuals, objects, or events that belong to the same category) and, based on that information, draws conclusions about the wider population represented by that sample. Inferential statistics also provides tools for ensuring that such conclusions are accurate and reliable.

Statistics are compiled and used to analyze trends in a wide range of areas, from employment to imports and exports to rainfall. Statistical analysis is a vital tool for all empirical sciences (meaning sciences that use observation and experiments), as well as for industry and management and popular culture.

Background
In the nineteenth century, the field of statistics consisted mainly of collecting huge amounts of data. State agencies and private organizations gathered information on topics as wide-ranging as agricultural yields, poverty, suicide, the height of mountaintops, and daily rainfall. However, there were few meaningful ways to analyze and compare these data.

Toward the end of the 1800s, the method of sampling (collecting information from a subset of a population, which represents the entire population) came into use. An early form of sampling was called "purposeful sampling"; it involved the careful construction of a subset intended to mimic the entire population. Purposeful sampling was eventually replaced by random sampling, the random selection of a subset of a population (such as choosing every tenth name on a list or measuring the height of every tenth plant in a field).

mean: a concept used to describe "average," found by adding all of the numbers in a set and dividing by the number of numbers.

population: a complete set of individuals, objects, or events that belong to the same category.

sample: a subset of a population that is representative of the entire population.

standard deviation: a measure used to determine how far, and in what numbers, measurements in a sample differ from the mean, or average.

variance: a measure of how far the data deviates from the mean, as compared to the sample size.

Eugenicists pioneer statistical methods

Much of the early development of statistical methods was done by eugenicists, scientists attempting to improve the human race through selective breeding (e.g., encouraging higher birth rates among wealthy people and lowering birth rates among or sterilizing people with mental illnesses or other "undesirable" characteristics). Eugenicists used statistical methods to study a wide variety of traits, from skull size to intelligence to eye color, of people from different ancestries.

One of the best-known early eugenicist-statisticians was Francis Galton (1822–1911) of England. Galton, who invented the term "eugenics" (from the Greek *eugenes,* meaning "wellborn") in 1883, supported government regulation of marriage partners based on the traits of the individuals. During a 1885 study comparing the height of children with the average height of their parents, Galton developed the concept of regression. Regression is a way to determine the expected value of one variable (in this case, a child's height) by looking at the known values of other variables (the average height of the parents). He later came up with the concept of correlation, a way to determine the statistical dependence (or close relationship) between variables.

British statistician **Karl Pearson** (1857–1936; see biography in this chapter), another leading eugenicist, advanced statistical theory to such a degree that he became known as the father of statistics. In the 1890s Pearson was inspired by one of Galton's studies of heredity (the transmission of inherited traits from parents to offspring) to develop a mathematical method for testing the precision of correlation. In other words, Pearson could determine whether an apparent linkage between two variables was mere chance or whether it had a solid connection that could withstand thorough testing. Today, correlation is widely used in medical tests (in comparing rates of smoking and lung cancer to determine how closely they are linked, for example).

Pearson later established the concept of "standard deviation," a measure used to determine how far, and in what numbers, measurements in a sample differ from the mean (average). Standard deviation can also be described as finding the average variance (a measure of how far the data deviates from the mean, or average) within a sample.

Fisher brings statistics into the modern era

British statistician and geneticist Sir Ronald Aylmer Fisher (1890–1962), who also took an interest in eugenics, was a central figure in the founding of modern statistics. In the 1920s, while studying sixty-six years' worth of agricultural research data at a laboratory north of London, Fisher came up with new techniques for experimentation and analysis. He set out three basic principles necessary to obtain reliable data that are still applied to experimentation today: randomization (the process of selecting a subset of a population in which each individual has an equal chance of being chosen), replication (the ability to use the same methods and get similar results in repeated experiments), and local control (the comparison only of subjects with fixed mathematical relationships).

British mathematician Karl Pearson, who became known as the father of statistics. (Reproduced by permission of Mathematisches Forschungsinstitute Oberwolfach.)

Fisher also developed a method of constructing experiments so that the statistician could examine multiple factors and answer several questions at once. (This was in contrast to traditional experimental methods, which varied only one factor in each experiment, a much less efficient method.) His technique was to divide each experiment into a series of mini-experiments, each of which was sufficiently different to guarantee unique outcomes. Using Fisher's method, it was not only possible to conduct experiments

A census is conducted in the United States every ten years. Results of a census tell much information about the nation's population, such as the number of people in each household and the age, race, and gender of each. It also indicates the distribution of people by age group, geographic area, and racial background. (Reproduced by permission of AP/Wide World Photos.)

more rapidly, but also to study the interactions between variables. Fisher published two landmark textbooks: *Statistical Methods for Research Workers* (1925) and *Statistical Methods and Scientific Inference* (1956).

Impact

The field of statistics expanded so greatly throughout the twentieth century that it has entered almost every area of society. Some of the fields that rely heavily on statistical studies include public health, medical research, marketing and quality control in business, weather forecasting, polls and surveys, sports, the entertainment industry, and insurance. Agriculturalists use statistical methods to decide how much of a given crop to produce, store owners use them to decide how much of which products to stock, and political candidates use them to determine how voters feel about various issues. Researchers in almost every division of the biological and social sciences have adopted the techniques and procedures developed in statistics.

One use of statistics with which people are most familiar is the census, an official tally of the population, including details such as age, gender, and occupation. The United States, along with many other countries, conducts a census every ten years. It is typically carried out through a mailed questionnaire. The general form, which is the one most people receive, asks about the number of people in the household and the age, race, and gender of each. A sample of the population receives a longer form that asks for more detailed information: profession, income, the number of cars they own, and so on. The information gained from a census describes a nation's population, economy, living arrangements (such as nuclear family, extended family, or nonrelated individuals living in a given household), as well as the distribution of people by age group, geographic area, and racial background.

☐ THE EMERGENCE OF WOMEN IN MATHEMATICS

Overview

Throughout most of history, women have been largely left out of the world of mathematics. Before the twentieth century, almost every institute of higher learning denied women entry, and mathematical societies barred them from membership. Despite these barriers, a handful of women mathematicians over the centuries contributed to the field. Some gained token recognition or limited access to mathematical facilities, while others were ignored or shunned. Some women mathematicians made great discoveries in the field while the credit for their work went to males. And at least one outspoken female mathematician and scientist was killed. The powerful intelligence and bravery of these women paved the way for the twentieth century's acceptance of women in mathematics.

Background

The earliest known female contributor to mathematics—and the only known important female scholar of ancient times—was Hypatia (c. 370–415 C.E.). Hypatia was the director of the school of philosophy at Alexandria, the great center of learning in ancient Egypt. She is credited with having invented or helped to invent the astrolabe (an instrument used to observe the positions of stars), the hydrometer (an instrument used to measure specific gravity, the density of a substance relative to the density of water), and the hydroscope (an instrument used to observe objects underwater). Hypatia was also the first mathematician to develop the idea of conic sections, an important concept in geometry that relates to the shapes formed when planes intersect curved surfaces. At the age of forty-five, Hypatia was murdered by a mob that was angered by her independence and intelligence, as well as by her political and religious connections.

In the eighteenth and nineteenth centuries, a series of female mathematicians left their marks on the field despite the difficulties in their way. French mathematician Emilie de Breteuil (1706–1749), as the wife of the Marquis du Châtelet, a French nobleman, had access to the finest tutors. She translated the discoveries of English mathematician Sir Isaac Newton (1642–1727) into French and added her own "Algebraical Commentary." She also published a textbook on physics that few at the time believed could have been written by a woman; rumors claimed it was actually written by one of Breteuil's male colleagues.

Another Frenchwoman, Sophie Germain (1776–1831), is considered one of the founders of mathematical physics. Although the Polytechnique School in Paris refused to admit female students, Germain studied books from her father's library and took correspondence courses (courses taught by mail) from the school. Germain is best known for developing mathematical equations describing the movement of elastic surfaces (surfaces that return to their original shape when the forces that are deforming them are removed; an example would be a rubber band, which snaps back to its original shape when the person stretching it lets go).

In the 1820s, the Scottish woman Mary Somerville (1780–1872) wrote a landmark paper on the magnetic properties of violet light despite having very little formal training. And Russian mathematician Sonya Kovalevskaya (1850–1891), known for her work on differential equations and other branches of theoretical mathematics, found university doors closed to her—both as a student and as a teacher—in Germany and Russia. (She ultimately found a teaching position at the University of Stockholm in Sweden.) In 1874 Kovalevskaya wrote a doctoral dissertation, which she submitted to the University of Göttengin in Germany. Although she was granted a doctorate, it was not considered "official" since she was not enrolled in classes at the school.

Early twentieth-century mathematicians
Conditions for women in mathematics began to improve in the late nineteenth century and early twentieth century. At that time a handful of uni-

versities—most notably the mathematical institute of the University of Göttengin (an internationally famous center of mathematics)—began allowing women in their Ph.D. programs. The first woman to go through Göttengin's doctoral program and receive a Ph.D. (in 1896) was Englishwoman **Grace Emily Chisholm Young** (1868–1944; see biography in this chapter). (Young came to Göttengin because English universities did not admit women.) In 1905 Young published a textbook on geometry that established several important geometric patterns that are still used in math classes today.

Emmy Amalie Noether (1882–1935; see biography in this chapter) was also one of the first women to attend classes at Göttengin. In the early 1900s, when Germany passed a law requiring all universities in the country to admit women, Noether transferred to Erlangen University, where her father was a professor. Noether earned her Ph.D. there in 1907, graduating at the top of her class. She wrote her dissertation on abstract algebra, listing systems of more than 300 covariant forms (entities having fixed mathematical relationships). Although she had earned her degree, when Noether tried to gain employment the university in Erlangen told her that the male students would not accept a female instructor.

Noether returned to Göttengin in 1915 to work with her friend, the famous German mathematician **David Hilbert** (1862–1943; see biography in this chapter), to determine the mathematics underlying what German-born American physicist Albert Einstein (1879–1955) later described as the general theory of relativity (a theory stating that gravity is a result of curved space-time, a four-dimensional construct that unites the three dimensions of space with time). Eventually, with Hilbert's help, Noether began teaching at the school. She became so famous as a lecturer that students from throughout Europe came to hear her speak. Noether continued her important work in abstract algebra and other mathematical areas and became one of the most noted mathematicians of her time. She was forced to leave Germany in 1933 because of her Jewish heritage (see essay The Devastation of Mathematics in Hitler's Germany in this chapter) and accepted a teaching position at Bryn Mawr, a women's college in Pennsylvania. She died there two years later.

Distinguished mathematician Grace Chisolm Young. Young was the first woman to get an official Ph.D. in Germany. (Reproduced by permission of Ms. Sylvia Wiegand.)

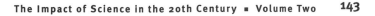

Olga Taussky-Todd leaves her mark on mathematics

Austrian-born American mathematician **Olga Taussky-Todd** (1906–1995; see biography in this chapter) earned her Ph.D. in 1930 at the University of Vienna. Taussky-Todd, who was twenty-four years younger than Noether, then worked with Noether at Göttengin and later at Bryn Mawr. (Like Noether, Taussky-Todd was Jewish and was forced to flee Germany after Adolf Hitler [1889–1945] came to power.) Taussky-Todd and Noether traveled together to England several times in the early 1930s to discuss their research with Albert Einstein.

Taussky-Todd's main focus of research was matrix theory (the study of sets of numbers arranged in columns and rows, which are subject to operations such as addition or multiplication according to certain rules) and its application to emerging computer technology. In 1957 the California Institute of Technology hired her to teach, and in 1971 she became the institution's first female full professor. She became a professor emeritus (an honorary position for a retired professor) in 1981. Taussky-Todd wrote more than 200 papers and received numerous awards during her career.

Prominent American mathematicians

A number of American-born women were also prominent in mathematics throughout the twentieth century. Anna Pell Wheeler (1883–1966) contributed to the study of integral equations (equations involving integrals with dependent variables) and other advanced concepts of calculus. She completed her undergraduate work at the University of South Dakota and received a fellowship to study mathematics at Göttengin. She returned to the United States and completed her Ph.D. at the University of Chicago in 1909. Wheeler spent most of her productive years at Bryn Mawr, where she eventually became head of the mathematics department. She was one of the first women to make presentations at meetings of the American Mathematical Society.

Another female pioneer of mathematics in the United States, Olive Clio Hazlett (1890–1974), earned her Ph.D. in mathematics at the University of Chicago in 1915. She spent most of her career at the University of Illinois, teaching calculus, trigonometry, geometry, and advanced algebra. She also wrote seventeen research papers on a variety of algebraic subjects, more than any other American woman mathematician before 1940.

Grace Murray Hopper (1906–1992) was an American mathematician who put her intellect to work on computer science. Hopper received her Ph.D. from Yale University in 1934, and after teaching for a period at Vassar College she joined the U.S. Navy, eventually rising to the rank of rear admiral. In the early 1940s Hopper wrote programs for the first American electronic computer, the Mark I. In the late 1940s, while working at the Remington Rand Corporation (later renamed the Sperry-Rand Corporation), she

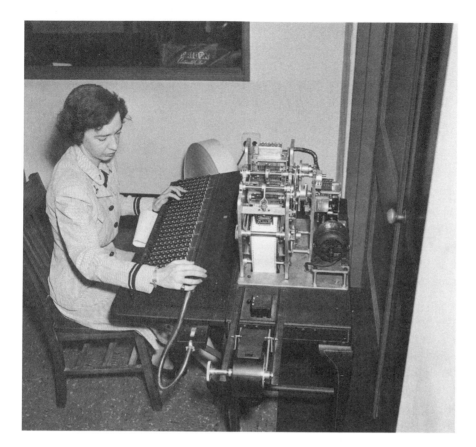

American admiral and computer scientist Grace Hopper was a pioneer in data processing. (Reproduced by permission of the Corbis Corporation.)

helped design the first commercially available electronic computer, the UNI-VAC (see essay The Development of Computational Mathematics in this chapter). In the 1950s, Hopper created FLOW-MATIC, the first programming language written in symbols (numbers and abbreviations for English-language words), and helped develop COBOL (Common Business Oriented Language), a programming language that uses entire words and phrases.

Julia Bowman Robinson (1919–1985; see biography in this chapter) was a prominent mathematician who devoted her career to number theory methodology and solving mathematical logic problems. Robinson, who earned a Ph.D. at the University of California, Berkeley, in 1948 and later became a full professor there, solved mathematical puzzles that had stumped other mathematicians for decades. In 1982 Robinson became the first female president of the American Mathematical Society.

Association for Women in Mathematics founded
In 1971, mathematicians Alice T. Schafer (1915–) and Mary Gray (1938–) founded the Association for Women in Mathematics (AWM), a nonprofit

organization that encourages women in the mathematical sciences. The AWM was started by a group of women who were attending a meeting of the American Mathematical Society. At that time, women faced open job discrimination in mathematics, particularly at universities. Many mathematics departments had no full-time female professors. When women were hired, it was in low-ranking, often temporary positions, and they received less pay than male professors. Women were also underrepresented in the student bodies of major universities. (Princeton University, for example, only started allowing women into its mathematics graduate program in 1968.)

The AWM, according to its Web site, has grown to more than 4,100 members worldwide. The organization sponsors workshops, offers a lecture series, and provides job placement services for its members. It also publishes a newsletter and periodic reports regarding women's access to mathematical careers, the current accomplishments of women mathematicians, and the contributions of women mathematicians throughout history.

Impact

By the end of the twentieth century, women throughout North America and Europe were recognized as important contributors to mathematics and had assumed leadership positions in mathematical societies. Women had also made great strides in employment in industry, computer science, and other technical areas. At university mathematics departments, however, women faculty members were still underrepresented.

In the mid-1990s, while women earned about one-quarter of new mathematics Ph.D.s in the United States, there were almost no tenured (a status that virtually guarantees a person will not be fired) female mathematics professors at the nation's top five mathematics departments. This is significant because universities with leading math programs have access to resources, prestige, and power, and they influence the direction of math research. At American universities, the average starting salaries for female mathematics faculty fell during the first half of the 1990s, while salaries stayed the same for new male mathematics professors. In addition, there were relatively few women in tenure-track and tenured positions, as well as in postdoctoral positions (jobs given to academics who have just earned their Ph.D.s).

☐ THE EMERGENCE OF AFRICAN AMERICANS IN MATHEMATICS

Overview

In the twentieth century, African Americans began to overcome the obstacles that had kept them out of mathematics. In the year 2000, about 1 percent of all mathematicians who held Ph.D.s in the United States were African Americans, and one-fourth of those were women. While that number is quite low, especially considering that African Americans represent nearly 13 percent of the U.S. population (according to the 2000 census), keep in mind that African Americans' access to doctoral programs only became widespread in the second half of the 1900s.

During the nearly 250 years of slavery in the United States, which ended after the Civil War (1861–65), it was illegal to educate slaves. Many leading white Americans, including President Thomas Jefferson (1743–1826), believed that blacks were "mathematically inferior." And for one hundred years after the Civil War, most educational facilities throughout the nation were segregated (separated by race), and there were few opportunities in higher education for African Americans.

Throughout the twentieth century, only about 300 African Americans earned advanced degrees in mathematics. Some of the most prominent among them are mentioned in this essay.

Background

The recorded history of African American involvement in mathematics typically begins with Benjamin Banneker (1731–1806), a self-taught mathematician, astronomer, and land surveyor. Banneker, a free black who lived during a time when most black people were slaves, built his own clock and published an annual almanac (a book containing information about the weather and other facts about the natural world) that was often used by farmers to help in growing crops. In 1792 Banneker joined a three-person surveying team led by French-born American engineer Major Pierre-Charles L'Enfant (pronounced lawn-FAWN; 1754–1825); their task was to survey the land where the new national capital—the District of Columbia—would be built. When L'Enfant abandoned the project, taking the plans for the new city with him, Banneker supposedly reproduced the plans from memory.

The first known African American mathematics faculty member at a college or university was Charles Reason (1818–1893). Reason was born in New York City to West Indies immigrants and showed a talent for math at an early age. When he was just fourteen years old, he got a job as a high school teacher. (Later, in response to charges that African American teachers were poorly trained, he founded a school for teachers.) From 1849 to 1852 Reason taught at the largely white Central College in Cortland County, New York. He later became principal at Philadelphia's Institute for Colored Youth and principal of New York City's School No. 6. In addition to being a mathematician and teacher, Reason was an abolitionist (a person who fought to end slavery) and a supporter of education for African American youth.

In 1925, Elbert Frank Cox (1895–1969) became the first African American to earn a Ph.D. in mathematics. (By way of comparison, the first mathematics Ph.D. earned by *anyone* in the United States was awarded in 1862; in 1925 there were a total of twenty-eight Ph.D.s in mathematics given out nationwide.) Cox grew up in Indiana; his father had done graduate studies at Indiana University and worked as a school principal. Cox earned his undergraduate degree at Indiana University in 1917, and after serving in the army during World War I (1914–18), he applied to graduate school at Cornell University. Cornell was, at the time, one of only seven universities in the United States offering a doctoral program in mathematics. After earning his Ph.D., Cox taught for several years at West Virginia State College. He then took a position at Howard University (a leading all-African-American institution) and remained there until he retired in 1965. For five years he served as chairman of Howard's mathematics department.

Regarded as perhaps the greatest African American mathematician, David Blackwell has explored several different fields of mathematics while making major contributions in the application of game theory. (Reproduced by permission of Mr. David Blackwell.)

David Blackwell: The most famous black mathematician

In the forty-five years after Cox received his Ph.D., another three dozen African Americans earned doctorates in mathematics. The most famous was **David Blackwell** (1919–; see biography in this chapter), who earned his Ph.D. at the University of Illinois in 1941. Blackwell spent ten years teaching at Howard University (along with Elbert Cox), and from 1954 to 1989 he taught at the University of California, Berkeley. While at Berkeley, Blackwell spent periods of time as chair of the statistics department.

Blackwell, while interested in several branches of mathematics, focused mainly on theoretical statistics (see essay Advances in the Field of Statistics in this chapter). He made important contributions to Bayesian statistical analysis (a method of using observed data to estimate probability, named after English mathematician Thomas Bayes [1702–1761]), dynamic programming (a system of mathematical reasoning that analyzes decision-making processes by starting with the best possible outcome and working backward), and game theory (the branch of mathematics concerned with analyzing conflict situations; see essay The Development of Game Theory in this chapter). Throughout his career, Blackwell published more than ninety papers on various mathematical topics and served as an advisor to more than fifty mathematics graduate students. Blackwell was the first African American elected to join the prominent National Academy of Sciences and the first African American president of the American Statistical Society.

Black women in mathematics

The first African American women earned Ph.D.s in mathematics in 1949 and 1950 (several African American women had received master's degrees in math in the first half of the twentieth century). By the end of the 1970s, another twenty black women had earned their doctorates in the field. Throughout the 1980s and 1990s, the number of African American women who earned Ph.D.s in mathematics each year remained in the single digits. In 1999, for instance, of the 1,119 math Ph.D.s awarded across the country, five went to African American women. The year before, African American women had earned seven. Mathematicians and educators attribute the slow entry of African American women and girls into mathematics to a lack of encouragement, race and gender discrimination, and a shortage of African American female teachers at colleges and universities to serve as role models.

The first African American woman to earn a Ph.D. in math, from Yale University in 1949, was Evelyn Boyd Granville (1924–). After receiving her Ph.D., Granville spent one year working as a research assistant at the New York University Institute of Mathematics. She then applied to teach at white universities but was turned down by all of them. From 1950 to 1952, Granville taught at the all-African-American Fisk University in Nashville, Tennessee, where two of her students, Vivienne Malone Mayes and Etta Zuber Falconer, went on to earn Ph.D.s in mathematics. Granville later found employment in industry, and in 1967 she was hired as a full professor at California State University in Los Angeles. She remained there until her retirement in 1984 and then taught at Texas College in Tyler from 1985 to 1988; in 1990 she began teaching at the University of Texas at Tyler as a visiting professor. Granville is the author of several books on mathematics education.

Evelyn Granville became one of the first two African American women to earn a Ph.D. in mathematics. Granville went on to a career not only as an educator but also as a distinguished applied mathematician in the field of aerospace technology. (Reproduced by permission of the University of Texas at Tyler.)

Marjorie Lee Browne (1914–1979) completed her dissertation the same year as Granville (1949) but did not receive her Ph.D. until the following year. Browne earned her bachelor's degree in mathematics from Howard University in 1935 and her master's degree (1939) and doctorate from the University of Michigan. After earning her Ph.D., Browne took a teaching position at the all-African-American North Carolina Central University, where she remained until her death. At least four of her students went on to earn Ph.D.s in mathematics. Browne also ran summer institutes to improve the mathematics education of high school teachers and published several papers on the teaching of advanced mathematics.

One of the most influential African American women mathematicians is **Etta Zuber Falconer** (1933–; see biography in this chapter). Born in Tupelo, Mississippi, Falconer received her bachelor's degree from Fisk University in 1953 and her master's degree from the University of Wisconsin in 1954. After teaching at various schools for ten years, she enrolled in the Ph.D. program in mathematics at Emory University in Atlanta, Georgia, graduating in 1969. Falconer spent most of her teaching career at the all-African-American Spelman College in Atlanta, rising to the rank of chair of the department of mathematics. In 1982 Falconer went back to school and earned a master's degree in computer science from Atlanta University. During the 1980s Falconer instituted several programs at Spelman to help undergraduates prepare for graduate studies, including the National Aeronautic and Space Administration (NASA) Women in Science Program and the NASA Undergraduate Science Research Program.

Marjorie Lee Browne was one of the first African American women to earn a Ph.D. Trained as a topologist (a branch of mathematics that deals with geometric aspects of spaces and shapes), Browne made her greatest contributions in teaching and university administration. (Reproduced by permission of Ms. Patricia Kenschaft.)

Impact

While individual African Americans distinguished themselves in mathematics throughout the twentieth century, as a group they have seen limited progress. According to the American Mathematical Society, between 1993 and 2000, 4,230 Ph.D.s in mathematics were awarded to U.S. citizens. Of those, just 72, or 1.7 percent, went to African Americans. African American mathematics professors at American universities are almost nonexistent. And those few African American professors are less likely than whites or Asians to be full professors, more likely to teach at junior or liberal arts colleges than major universities, and on average receive lower salaries than their white colleagues.

Another indication of African Americans' current status in mathematics is reflected in the standardized test scores of schoolchildren. The 2000 National Assessment of Educational Programs, the only test that measures student achievement nationwide, found a large gap between the achievements of African American (and Hispanic) children and their white or Asian counterparts in both math and reading. Furthermore, little progress was made in closing that gap between 1992 and 2000.

Some experts argue that the slow progress of African Americans in mathematics reflects the relatively short period of time in which African Americans have enjoyed opportunities in higher education and employment. Only the future will tell whether the African American mathematicians who broke new ground in the twentieth century have made those opportunities more widely available.

☐ NEW MATH IN AMERICAN PUBLIC SCHOOLS

Overview

New Math, launched in the early 1960s in the United States, was a method of teaching mathematics that stressed conceptual (intuitive) understanding of the foundations of mathematics. It downplayed the memorization of math facts and formulas, which had long been the focus of mathematics education. New Math aimed to teach children basic mathematical truths that they could then apply to a variety of specific problems. Introduced in an era when the United States was competing with other countries for mathematical superiority, New Math was supposed to prepare the minds of young mathematicians for the challenges of the twentieth century.

New Math, however, enjoyed a short and bumpy lifespan in U.S. public schools. The new teaching methods proved confusing to educators and parents who had learned mathematics through the traditional methods. In addition, educators, administrators, and parents disagreed on the goals and objectives of math education. Polls in the early 1970s showed that Americans favored a "back to basics" approach, and by the end of that decade New Math had almost disappeared from schools.

In 1989 the National Council of Teachers of Mathematics (NCTM) developed a "newer" New Math, usually called "standards math." More than forty states began using standards math during the 1990s. Standards math emphasized teamwork, the use of three-dimensional objects, and problem solving in real-life situations. Like New Math, the "new New Math" (as stan-

The Algebra Project

Robert Moses.
(Reproduced by permission of
Ceaser Photography.)

The failure of African American youth to improve their math skills is a great cause for concern in this country. One person particularly alarmed by this trend is Robert Moses, who in the early 1960s organized a voting-rights campaign for African Americans in Mississippi. (African Americans did not gain the right to vote in many parts of the country until the Voting Rights Act passed in 1965.) Over the past two decades, Moses has been using his expertise at community organizing to develop a math literacy program aimed mainly at African American youth: the Algebra Project (A.P.). Moses argues that strong training in mathematics is the key to entry into today's high-tech job market—and he believes that radical reform of the education system is the only way to accomplish that for underprivileged kids.

dards math is sometimes called) has proved controversial. As the 1990s came to a close, supporters and critics of standards math were engaged in a conflict over the best way to teach math that has been dubbed the "math wars."

Background
The need for a new way of teaching mathematics became clear during World War II (1939–45), when American soldiers had more difficulty than their European counterparts operating radar and other advanced technologies. Another event that affected mathematics teaching was the emigration of many European scientists and mathematicians who fled Adolf Hitler's

As described by Moses in his 2001 book *Radical Equations: Math Literacy and Civil Rights* (co-written with Charles Cobb, senior writer at the allAfrica.com information agency), "The work of the A.P. is to help close the gap between universal free public education and universal completion of a college preparatory math sequence in high school." Moses founded the A.P. with the prize money from his MacArthur "genius" award in 1982. He came up with the idea for the A.P. when his eldest daughter, Maisha, wanted to take algebra in eighth grade, but her Cambridge public school did not offer the course. Moses, who has a Ph.D. in philosophy from Harvard University, volunteered to teach algebra to his daughter and a handful of other interested students.

Since that time, the A.P. has spread to twenty-eight communities in ten states and reaches ten thousand students. It operates in major cities such as Chicago, Atlanta, Cleveland, San Diego, Milwaukee, Louisville, Oakland, San Francisco, and Los Angeles, and it covers large portions of the rural South, from the Mississippi Delta to North Carolina. In many of the schools where the A.P. is in place, students' math scores on standardized tests have improved tremendously. The key to the success of the A.P. is two-fold: enlisting the support of the community and teaching math in a way that makes it relevant to students' lives.

(1889–1945) forces (see essay The Devastation of Mathematics in Hitler's Germany in this chapter) and settled in the United States. The refugee scientists were central to developing the strategies and tools used to win the war. A third factor emphasizing the need for improved mathematics education came in the early 1950s, when the high-tech era began with the introduction of computers, nuclear energy, cable television, jet engines, and the like. These new technologies caused industrial jobs to become less physical and more intellectual in nature.

Also in the wake of World War II, the United States entered a period of tense relations with the Soviet Union (now Russia and surrounding nations) called the Cold War. The Cold War involved struggles for superiority on all fronts: military, economic, political, and intellectual. As a result, a well-educated populace was seen as essential. The stakes for math education in the United States were raised even higher in October 1957, when the Soviet Union launched the first artificial satellite to successfully orbit the Earth, the *Sputnik 1*. That event set in motion the space race, the contest between the United States and the Soviet Union for superiority in space travel and exploration. With the United States seemingly falling behind the Soviets in the space race, the nation's poor mathematics standings became a national crisis. Public schools were blamed for not producing enough mathematicians and scientists to meet the current demand.

The adoption of New Math

In the years before New Math, American students were divided into groups for math instruction depending on their abilities. They learned mathematical concepts through repetition, memorization, and timed drills. Many students came to dislike mathematics, seeing it as something that only the smartest students could master. In the years just before New Math was adopted, one-third of all students had stopped taking math classes by ninth grade.

The New Math approach, developed by the National Science Foundation in 1957, was being used in classrooms throughout the United States by the early 1960s. Rather than focusing on solving lists of math problems, New Math focused on set theory (operations on sets of numbers grouped by their characteristics and properties) and abstract (theoretical) mathematical laws. It also taught the binary (base two) number system, assuming that Americans would be expected to program their own computers. However, this became unnecessary with the development of pre-packaged computer software that reduced computer operation to pointing and clicking.

The demise of New Math

Despite education experts' initial enthusiasm for New Math, concerns quickly arose about the program. While impressive on paper, it proved difficult for teachers to present in the classroom. Part of the problem with New Math was that teachers had little training in the new methods and were struggling to understand them even as they used them to teach students. Another problem was that New Math was foreign to parents. Even though New Math classes for parents were offered in some areas, many parents complained that they could no longer help their children with their homework. To many parents, the New Math methods were unnecessarily complicated. In addition, parents became concerned that their children were not learning the basic concepts of math, such as the multiplication tables.

Another strike against New Math was that it was put in place at the same time as schools started using standardized tests to measure student progress. The new tests increased the pressure on schools to improve mathematics skills in students; when this improvement failed to materialize, New Math became a convenient scapegoat.

Mathematicians and educators began to criticize New Math in academic journals in 1962. A five-year study, begun in 1962 and published in 1967, showed that American students continued to trail students in other Western nations in math skills. By the early 1970s, many schools had given up New Math in favor of a "back to basics" approach favoring traditional methods. The problems of New Math were laid out in the widely read 1973 book *Why Johnny Can't Add: The Failure of The New Math* by math professor Morris Kline.

A junior high school student in the 1960s, explaining to two adults the principle of multiplying by one, one of the several rules of the "new math." (Reproduced by permission of AP/Wide World Photos.)

The "new" New Math

Two decades after a return to traditional math—with no improvement in students' scores—experts again began looking for ways to make math more meaningful to kids. The result was the reformed mathematical standards, a set of fifty statements of what students should learn, set out by the NCTM in 1989. Members of the NCTM recognized the benefits of some of the New Math concepts, and they concluded that the 1960s' program had failed in part because of a lack of teacher training. The NCTM's 1989 program called for educators to receive extensive training in the new methods.

Like New Math, standards math plays down the importance of memorization and math drills. Instead, standards math emphasizes "experiential learning," in which students work in groups to figure out answers for themselves. Also central to standards math is teaching students mapping and graphing skills; probability and statistics; and how to use calculators, explain their answers, and solve multi-step problems. Standards math also employs "manipulatives," three-dimensional objects such as snap-together blocks, to build models of mathematical concepts, and uses computer simulations to teach students the visual aspects of math problems. In addition to solving math problems with pencil and paper, students use real-world experiences to learn about numbers, such as measuring the length of their playground and creating graphs based on the numbers and types of sandwiches brought for lunch.

The debate over standards math

Standards math was introduced in several states in the 1990s, with partial funding from the U.S. Congress. By 1997 it was being used in about half of all U.S. public high schools and about 10 percent of U.S. public elementary schools. Standards math has been controversial, attracting both defenders and critics. People who favor standards math say that it improves strategic thinking and teaches students to problem-solve in groups, similar to the way research scientists and mathematicians operate. Standards math supporters also argue that the math of the past was intended to prepare an elite group of students for college, whereas standards math is aimed at training all students for the demands of the workplace. Those who oppose standards math claim that it fails to adequately teach kids the basics and that it "dumbs down" the subject. They call it "the new New Math," "Fuzzy Math," and even "Rainforest Math" (referring to the social issues frequently addressed in standards math textbooks).

One point of disagreement between supporters and opposers of standards math is that it typically gives partial credit to encourage students who attempt to solve a problem but get it wrong. While supporters of standards math claim that the practice boosts the self-esteem of kids who are typically scared away by math, critics argue that in mathematics only right answers count and students should be judged on their answers alone. The emphasis on teamwork has also been debated; while some claim that students can learn from one another while tackling problems together, others argue that it allows weak students to slide through while strong students do all the work. And while standards math critics complain about the dismissal of the multiplication tables and other traditional tools, the NCTM insists that the standards have been distorted and that they never called for throwing out the multiplication tables.

Impact

New Math of the 1960s, as well as the standards math of the 1990s, raised questions about what American public schools should teach and how they should teach it. The "math wars" over math reform movements have divided communities, seen the formation of parent lobbying groups, and caused angry educators to resign. But most of all, the math wars have made it clear that while most people agree that American public education needs improvement, there are many different ideas about how that should happen. At the end of the twentieth century, while the method of teaching mathematics remained controversial, U.S. students continued to lag behind the rest of the industrialized world in math competency.

◻ BIOGRAPHIES

◻ GEORGE DAVID BIRKHOFF (1884–1944)

American mathematician

George David Birkhoff is considered one of the most significant mathematicians of the twentieth century. He is best known for founding the modern theory of dynamical systems, the study of how separate motions in individual bodies are related, as well as the impact of the bodies on one another. He also advanced the mathematical disciplines of differential equations (equations involving differences between variables), relativity (the theory that all motion must be defined relative to a frame of reference and that space and time are relative, not absolute, concepts), quantum mechanics (physical principles used to describe submicroscopic phenomena), and the four-color theorem (the theory that any geographic map can be filled in using just four colors, so that no countries sharing a common border are the same color). He also developed a mathematical theory to explain the concept of beauty.

Studies mathematics at Harvard

Birkhoff, the eldest of six children, was born on March 21, 1884, to David Birkhoff, a physician, and Jane Gertrude (Droppers) Birkhoff. Birkhoff lived for two years in Overisel, Michigan, and then moved with his family to Chicago, where he spent most of his boyhood years.

Birkhoff began his undergraduate education at the University of Chicago in 1902, and the following year he transferred to Harvard University. He wrote his first mathematical paper, on number theory, while still an undergraduate and earned his bachelor's degree in 1905. The following year he completed his master's degree.

Birkhoff next returned to the University of Chicago to work on his doctorate. He wrote his dissertation on differential equations and in 1907 earned his Ph.D., graduating summa cum laude (with highest honors). Birkhoff then spent two years teaching mathematics at the University of Wisconsin. During that time he married Margaret Grafius, with whom he had three children. (One of his children, Garrett Birkhoff, went on to become a mathematics professor at Harvard.) From 1909 through 1912 Birkhoff worked as an assistant professor at Princeton University.

George David Birkhoff.
(Courtesy of the Library
of Congress.)

Proves Poincaré's theorem

Birkhoff spent the bulk of his career, from 1912 until his death in 1944, teaching at Harvard University. From 1935 to 1939 he served as dean of the Faculty of Arts and Science. At Harvard, Birkhoff trained several students who became influential mathematicians, such as Marston Morse (1892–1977), who specialized in calculus, and Marshall Stone (1903– 1989), who specialized in linear differential equations. Both Morse and Stone went on to teach at Harvard as well. Six of Birkhoff's students (a very large number for a single professor) were eventually elected to the prestigious National Academy of Sciences.

One of Birkhoff's greatest accomplishments came in 1913, when he proved a geometrical theorem proposed by noted French mathematician Jules-Henri Poincaré (1854–1912). That theorem looks at the trajectories (curved paths) and orbits of three bodies in space and the ways that each body affects the motions of the others. Throughout his career, Birkhoff continued to make significant contributions to the study of dynamical systems.

In 1931 Birkhoff offered another important proof, this one for the ergodic theorem. That theorem, which perplexed mathematicians for fifty years, concerns the behavior of large systems of bodies in motion (such as gas in a container). Specifically, it lays out the conditions necessary for such a system to reach equilibrium (a state of balance due to the equal actions of opposing forces).

Writings and professional accomplishments

Beginning in the 1920s, Birkhoff wrote extensively about mathematics and other scholarly pursuits. In his first book, *Relativity and Modern Physics* (1923), Birkhoff contributed his ideas to the growing field of relativity theory. He wrote *Dynamical Systems* in 1928, which outlined the fundamentals of this relatively new branch of knowledge. In 1933, inspired by his lifelong passion for poetry, music, and art, Birkhoff wrote *Aesthetic Measure*. In that book he attempted to reach a mathematical understanding of beauty. And Birkhoff published the textbook *Basic Geometry* in 1941, which was widely used in high school classrooms for years.

Birkhoff was an active member of the American Mathematical Society (AMS), serving as the group's vice president in 1919 and president from 1925 to 1926. From 1921 to 1924 Birkhoff was the editor of the AMS journal *Transactions of the American Mathematical Society*.

Throughout his career, Birkhoff presented numerous papers around the world, often in French—which he spoke fluently—and received numerous awards and honorary degrees. He was an elected member of the National Academy of Sciences, the American Philosophical Society, and the American Academy of Arts and Sciences. Birkhoff was made an officer of the French Legion of Honor in 1936 and was an honorary member of the Edinburgh Mathematical Society, the London Mathematical Society, the Peruvian Philosophic Society, and the Scientific Society of Argentina. He died of a heart attack in Cambridge, Massachusetts, on November 12, 1944.

◻ PAUL ERDÖS (1913–1996)

Hungarian mathematician

Paul Erdös (pronounced ER-dish) was one of the twentieth century's most brilliant, and most eccentric, mathematicians. Erdös, who specialized in number theory (the study of whole numbers and their relation to one another) and combinatorics (a branch of mathematics involving the arrangement of finite sets), made a career of traveling all over the world, hopping from one university or mathematical conference to the next. He would drop in on colleagues, sometimes unannounced, and lecture, banter, and write papers for weeks or months at a time.

Erdös was just as famous for posing problems as he was for solving them, and he encouraged mathematics students to answer problems he had not yet tackled. According to a March 29, 1999, *Time* magazine article about Erdös, "In a profession with no shortage of oddballs, he was the strangest."

Paul Erdös.
(Reproduced by permission of the Wolf Foundation.)

A child prodigy in an overprotective home

Erdös was born on March 26, 1913, in Budapest, Hungary. He was the third child born to high-school mathematics teachers Lajos and Anna Erdös. Erdös's two older sisters died of scarlet fever shortly before he was born, so his parents were very protective of him. Erdös was kept at home through his childhood and educated by private tutors. He was coddled so much, it was reported, that he did not butter his own bread until he was twenty-one years old and that, even after he became an adult, he never cut his own grapefruit or did his own laundry.

Erdös showed an early gift for mathematics, multiplying three- and four-digit numbers in his head at the age of three. When he was four years old, he began to explore the meaning of negative numbers. At the age of seventeen, Erdös entered the University of Budapest and four years later emerged with a Ph.D. in mathematics (it typically takes several years after finishing a four-year undergraduate degree to complete a Ph.D.). Erdös spent the following year in a postdoctoral fellowship at the University of Manchester in England.

Flees Nazi forces

Erdös, who was of Jewish background, found himself unable to return to Hungary after his time in England. The year was 1934, and the Nazi forces of Adolf Hitler (1889–1945; see essay The Devastation of Mathematics in Hitler's Germany in this chapter) threatened Jews throughout eastern Europe. As it turned out, four of Erdös's relatives were murdered during World War II (1939–45), and his father died of a heart attack in 1942.

The Erdös Number

As evidence of Paul Erdös's popularity in the math world, mathematicians assign themselves a number, known as an Erdös number, that is a measure of how closely connected they were with Erdös. An Erdös number of 1 conveys that the bearer co-wrote a paper with Erdös. If someone has a number of 2, that means he or she co-wrote a paper with someone who co-wrote a paper with Erdös. German-born American physicist Albert Einstein (1879–1955), for instance, had an Erdös number of 2. According to the Erdös Number Project Data Files (http://www.oakland.edu/~grossman/thedata.html), there were 507 people with an Erdös number of 1 and 6,419 people with an Erdös number of 2 in 2002.

Erdös first traveled to the United States but decided not to settle there permanently. He next sought a homeland in the section of Palestine that would become Israel in 1948. He eventually became a citizen of Israel, but he also kept his Hungarian citizenship.

Begins life of mathematics and travel

Erdös spent the rest of his life as a traveling mathematician, rapidly achieving fame for his sharp mind and endless energy. He had no home, no formal connection with any university, and no financial security. He also never married (his primary emotional attachment was to his mother, who sometimes traveled with him). Erdös was supported mainly by a small yearly stipend from the Hungarian Academy of Sciences.

Erdös's mode of operation was to arrive at the home of a colleague or at a university, announce that he would be staying for a period of time, and expect his hosts to house him, feed him, and do his laundry. In exchange, he would open his mind to them, providing endless mathematical challenges and conversations. Erdös also traveled to mathematical conferences around the world. He said he never suffered from jet lag and once remarked that he thought the perfect death would be to "fall over dead" while delivering a lecture.

Some of Erdös's favorite mathematical problems were those that appeared simple but actually were quite complex. He would often pose problems that he had not yet solved to younger mathematicians, offering them cash awards (from $10 to $3,000) for the solutions. In 1983 Erdös used the $50,000 purse that he received with the Wolf Prize in Mathematics to establish two scholarships in his parents' names.

Becomes depressed at mother's death

In 1971, the death of Erdös's mother sent the mathematician into a depression from which he never recovered. To cover up his sadness, he began taking amphetamines (stimulant drugs) that made him hyperactive and erratic. Despite the urging of friends, Erdös refused to treat his addiction.

Erdös continued his mathematical activities for twenty-five years after the death of his mother. On September 20, 1996, while attending a mathematics meeting in Warsaw, Poland, he had a heart attack and died—a scenario similar to what he had described as the perfect death.

◻ DAVID HILBERT (1862–1943)

German mathematician

In the early part of the twentieth century, David Hilbert was the world's best known and most influential mathematician. His contributions to number theory, geometry, and the logic of mathematics changed the field in profound and lasting ways. The twenty-three questions Hilbert posed at an international gathering of mathematicians in 1900 set the mathematical agenda for much of the twentieth century. At the peak of Hilbert's career, Nazi dictator Adolf Hitler (1889–1945) came to power in Germany and began to purge the nation of Jewish professors and other intellectuals. Hilbert watched the tragic unraveling of the University of Göttingen, at which he had spent most of his professional life building the math department into the world's center of mathematics (see essay The Devastation of Mathematics in Hitler's Germany in this chapter).

Upbringing and education

Hilbert was born on January 23, 1862, in Königsberg, East Prussia (then a German state; the town is now called Kaliningrad and is in Russia). His father, Otto, was a lawyer; the family took great pride in their high social standing and devout Protestantism. Hilbert in later years would anger his family by leaving the church and by forming a close association with Hermann Minkowski (1864–1909), a Jewish mathematician from the lower classes.

After completing primary school and high school, Hilbert entered the University of Königsberg in 1880. He graduated with a Ph.D. five years later and took a teaching post at the same university. In 1892 he married a woman named Käthe Jerosch (they later had one son); that same year he reached the rank of professor.

In 1895 Hilbert was lured to the prestigious University of Göttingen and made chair of the mathematics department. He remained there until he retired in 1930.

Redefines theory of invariants

Hilbert's early work as a mathematician was on the theory of invariants. Invariants are values that do not change when certain operations are performed on them. For instance, if all coefficients (numbers placed before [and multiplying] variable quantities, such as the "3" in the expression "3x") in an equation are doubled, the solution of the invariant equation remains the same. Previously, mathematicians had attempted to classify invariants by endless series of calculations—as evidenced by the pages filled with symbols in books on invariant theory.

Hilbert suggested that all that figuring was unnecessary and created a much simpler method of classifying invariants. His radical proposal was so unsettling to other mathematicians that virtually all research into invariant theory came to a standstill. Several years later invariant theory was revisited, and when mathematicians found that Hilbert's conclusions were accurate, they adopted his methods.

Assesses the state of number theory

In the early 1890s, Hilbert began a lifelong alliance with Russian-German mathematician Hermann Minkowski. In 1893, the German Mathematical Society hired Hilbert and Minkowski to summarize the current state of number theory (the study of positive and negative whole numbers and their relation to one another), the oldest branch of mathematics. Minkowski eventually withdrew from the project, but Hilbert continued to work on it, and in 1897 he wrote a paper titled *Zahlbericht* ("Commentary on Numbers"). In that paper, he advanced number theory to a more technical level and introduced new frameworks in which number theory research would take place during the twentieth century.

Re-assesses Euclidian geometry

Hilbert next set his sights on Euclidian geometry, the form of geometry developed by the Greek mathematician Euclid in the third century B.C.E. Hilbert examined the many untested axioms (statements accepted as true) in Euclidian geometry and discovered that Euclid had made several assumptions that were neither clearly explained nor backed up by proofs. This led Hilbert to argue that every axiom should be specifically proved.

In doing so, Hilbert changed not only the basis of geometry but also the entire philosophy of mathematics.

Presents list of twenty-three problems

In the year 1900, Hilbert made a historic address to the International Congress of Mathematicians in Paris in which he posed a set of twenty-three problems for mathematicians to solve in the twentieth century. Hilbert's list set the agenda for mathematicians around the world, and several of his problems kept mathematicians busy for decades.

Hilbert's first problem, for example, explored the relationship between two sets of numbers: real and rational (definitions follow). This problem arose from the theorem proven in the late nineteenth century by Russian-born German mathematician Georg Cantor (1845–1918) that the quantity of rational numbers (numbers that can be expressed exactly by a ratio of two integers) is the same as the quantity of whole (not fractional) numbers. Cantor also proved that the infinity of real numbers (rationals and irrationals combined) is larger than the infinity of rational numbers.

Hilbert's first problem asked the question of whether there are differences in the sizes of infinite sets between the real and rational numbers. In 1963, American mathematician Paul Cohen (1934–) concluded that the question cannot be answered by our axioms of set theory (operations on sets of numbers grouped by their characteristics and properties); that either answer is consistent with set theory.

Mathematician Hermann Minkowski. (Reproduced by permission of the Corbis Corporation.)

Clashes with German government

Hilbert had a series of disagreements with the German government throughout his career, beginning in World War I (1914–18), when he placed personal and professional commitments above nationalism (allegiance to one's country). During that period, when Germany and France were at war, Hilbert took the bold step of writing an obituary for a French colleague. He also refused to sign the "Declaration to the Cultural World," a document that claimed Germany was innocent of certain war crimes.

Hilbert's clashes with the German government became even worse after Hitler's rise to power in 1933. Hilbert condemned the firing of his

Jewish colleagues from the University of Göttingen and other learning institutions. Due to his old age, however, he refused to leave Germany and start a new career abroad, as many of his colleagues did. Hilbert died in Germany in 1943; only about a dozen people defied the Nazi regime and attended his funeral.

☐ EMMY AMALIE NOETHER (1882–1935)

German-born American mathematician

Emmy Amalie Noether overcame two forms of discrimination—against women and against Jews—to rise to the forefront of mathematics. Born at a time in which women were kept out of mathematics (see essay The Emergence of Women in Mathematics in this chapter), Noether first struggled for the right to study and then for the right to teach at institutions of higher learning. She conducted much of her groundbreaking work in mathematics in the shadow of leading male mathematicians. Around the time Noether was finally gaining acceptance in the German mathematics community, her career was interrupted by the rise to power of Adolf Hitler's (1889–1945) Nazi forces (see essay The Devastation of Mathematics in Hitler's Germany in this chapter). Forced to leave Germany, Noether took a position at an American university but died a short time later.

Emmy Amalie Noether. (Reproduced by permission of Archive Photos, Inc.)

Reared in an intellectual family

Noether was born on March 23, 1882, in Erlangen, Germany, to Max and Ida Kaufmann Noether. Max Noether was a popular professor of mathematics at the University of Erlangen and was noted for his work on the theory of algebraic functions. Emmy Noether had three younger brothers, one of whom became a mathematician and another of whom became a chemist.

Unlike her brothers, Noether was not allowed to attend college preparatory school (schools of advanced study were not open to women or girls at the time). She therefore took advantage of one of the few educational opportunities open to her and enrolled in a teachers' college for women, passing the Bavarian state teaching examinations in 1900.

Pushes for the right to an education

Still not satisfied with her education, Noether pressed for and was granted the right to attend lectures at the University of Erlangen. She also took classes at the University of Göttengin, which toward the end of the nineteenth century became one of the first institutions to open its doors to women. In 1904, when the University of Erlangen was required by a new law to admit women, Noether transferred to that school. She entered the doctoral program in mathematics and in 1907 completed her dissertation, graduating with highest honors.

Carves out professional niche

Although Noether had been granted a degree, she was unable to find work as a professor. From 1908 to 1915 she worked without pay at Erlangen, doing research and sometimes lecturing in place of her elderly and increasingly frail father. During that period she published six mathematical research papers.

In 1915 Noether moved to Göttengin at the invitation of her friend and former teacher, the famous mathematician **David Hilbert** (1862–1943; see biography in this chapter). Hilbert argued at faculty meetings that Noether's gender was no reason to deny her a position at the university. He was unsuccessful, however, and Noether was forced to rely on financial support from her family.

Noether worked with Hilbert on problems relating to what German-born American physicist Albert Einstein (1879–1955) later described as the general theory of relativity (a theory stating that gravity is a result of curved space-time, a four-dimensional construct that unites the three dimensions of space with time). Noether's particular area of expertise was "invariance under transformation," concepts that remain the same regardless of changes in space and time. She conducted groundbreaking research and developed theorems explaining the relationships between invariance (a quantity that remains unchanged by a given change in form) and equations of motion.

Obtains position as lecturer

While working with Hilbert, Noether often gave guest lectures in his classroom. She received no pay for the lectures, and Hilbert had to be listed as the official lecturer. Nonetheless, Noether gained a reputation among students as an enthusiastic and compelling instructor.

In 1919, University of Göttengin administrators finally made Noether an adjunct professor (connected with the university but not having permanent status). The thirty-seven-year-old received a small salary in return for teaching algebra, giving examinations, and supervising dissertations. She received neither benefits nor pension rights.

Noether also continued to conduct research, and in 1920 she published an important paper on abstract algebra. That paper came to the attention of noted German mathematician **Hermann Weyl** (1885–1955; see biography in this chapter), who called Noether's ideas "epoch-making." Weyl lobbied for Noether to receive a higher-status appointment at Göttengin, but he was unsuccessful.

Career cut short by Nazi reign

The year 1932 was a significant one in Noether's life: she turned fifty years old, received the coveted Alfred Ackermann-Teubner Memorial Prize for the advancement of mathematics, and was the only woman invited to lecture at a general session of the International Mathematical Congress. Noether's hard-earned success, however, was short-lived. In 1933 Adolf Hitler took power, and Noether was informed in that year that due to her Jewish heritage, she could no longer teach in Germany.

With assistance from the Emergency Committee in Aid of Displaced Foreign Scholars, a group formed in New York City by American academics to help their European colleagues who were being forced from their jobs, Noether came to the United States and accepted a faculty position at Bryn Mawr, an all-women's college in Pennsylvania. Her new career had hardly gotten started, however, when she developed a tumor on her uterus that required surgery. Noether died of complications from the surgery on April 14, 1935.

◻ SRINIVASA A. RAMANUJAN (1887–1920)

Indian mathematician

Srinivasa Ramanujan (pronounced SHRIN-i-vas-uh RAH-mah-noo-jen) was a largely self-taught mathematician who gained an international reputation for his ability to solve complex problems. His contributions to number theory (the study of positive and negative whole numbers and their relation to one another) have proved useful in physics, chemistry, computer programming, and other areas. In the early twentieth century, when almost all leading mathematicians were from Europe, Ramanujan put India on the mathematical map.

Childhood and education

Ramanujan was born on December 22, 1887, in his mother's home town of Erode in the Madras province of southern India. Ramanujan's father worked as a bookkeeper and clerk, and his mother boosted the family's modest income by singing religious songs at a nearby temple. Shortly after Ramanujan's birth, his family moved to Kumbakonam, also in southern India. Since Ramanujan did not speak until he was three years old, his family at first believed he was not a very bright child.

Ramanujan's amazing intellect became apparent, however, when he started attending school. At the age of ten, he received the highest scores in mathematics of any student in the school district; as a result, he was transferred to the high school. Ramanujan quickly became bored with high school studies as his mathematical abilities went beyond those of his teachers. By the age of twelve he had taught himself trigonometry from a book he borrowed from a college student.

Srinivasa Ramanujan. (Reproduced by permission of Mathematisches Forschunginstitut Oberwolfach.)

Becomes absorbed in mathematics

Before he graduated from high school, Ramanujan had become totally absorbed in mathematics. The book he credited with cementing his obsession was *Synopsis of Elementary Results in Pure and Applied Mathematics* by English mathematician George Shoobridge Carr. That book presented more than 5,000 mathematical formulas, equations, and results in algebra, geometry, trigonometry, and calculus, but it provided no explanations or proofs. Ramanujan put aside all other concerns and devoted himself to working out proofs for each problem.

In 1904, at the age of sixteen, Ramanujan entered the Government College in Kumbakonam on a fellowship. He was not successful in college, however, because his passion for mathematics kept him from studying for his other classes. He eventually switched to another college in Madras but continued to spend every waking hour working out mathematics problems in the notebook he always carried. As a result, he was unable to graduate. After giving up on college, Ramanujan disappeared from public view for a few years. It is believed that he spent that time wandering through the countryside, making mathematical notations in his notebook.

Marriage and employment

When Ramanujan was twenty-one years old, a marriage was arranged for him with the daughter of a distant relative, a young girl named Janaki.

(Arranged marriages were common at that time in India.) After they married on July 14, 1909, it was time for Ramanujan to find employment to support himself and his bride.

Ramanujan began his job hunt at the Indian Mathematical Society. There he met noted mathematician Ramachandra Rao and requested a small salary so he could continue his work on mathematics. Rao was impressed by Ramanujan and for a short time supported the young man himself. Rao eventually found Ramanujan a job as an accounts clerk. The work was not demanding, and it gave Ramanujan a small income while allowing him to pursue mathematics.

Explores avenues for mathematical advancement

In 1911 Ramanujan published his first paper, in the *Journal of the Indian Mathematical Society*. Realizing that far more advanced mathematics research was being conducted in England than in India, he started writing letters of introduction to mathematicians in England. After many discouraging responses, Ramanujan received a promising letter from number theorist Godfrey Harold Hardy (1877–1947), a fellow of Trinity College at Cambridge University. Hardy was impressed with the mathematical works Ramanujan had sent him—particularly a formula for estimating how many prime numbers came before a given number—and saw great potential in Ramanujan's bright but largely untrained mind. Hardy invited Ramanujan to come to England and offered him a scholarship to study at Trinity.

Ramanujan was hesitant to travel to England because of religious and dietary restrictions. In keeping with his Hindu religion, Ramanujan was a strict vegetarian. He doubted whether he could meet his dietary requirements in England. The question of whether to go was ultimately decided by Ramanujan's mother, who had a dream in which she was told that her son must meet his destiny. Thus in 1914 Ramanujan set sail for England.

Conducts research in England

Ramanujan spent five years in England, during which time he worked on some twenty papers with Hardy. Ramanujan's intuition and originality (and special talent for finding hidden patterns in series of numbers) meshed well with Hardy's classical mathematics training and methodical approach. The pair produced groundbreaking research on number theory, including a landmark paper on "highly composite numbers," numbers that can be evenly divided by many other numbers. Another paper, which proved especially useful to physicists, described the many ways a number can be expressed as the sum of other numbers.

While in England, Ramanujan finally earned his bachelor's degree (from Cambridge University in 1916). He also received numerous honors, including election to the Royal Society (England's most prominent scientific association) and a fellowship at Trinity College.

Sickness brings early death

By his fifth year in England, Ramanujan had become ill, lonely, and homesick. Weakened by an inadequate diet and the damp, chilly climate, Ramanujan contracted tuberculosis—then an incurable lung disease. In 1919 Ramanujan returned to India. He never recovered from his illness, however, and died one year later, on April 26, 1920. He was just thirty-two years old.

☐ JULIA BOWMAN ROBINSON (1919–1985)
American mathematician

Julia Bowman Robinson was a leading American mathematician of the twentieth century who specialized in number theory (the study of positive and negative whole numbers and their relation to one another) and its application to logic problems. She played a critical role in the solution of Hilbert's Tenth Problem. The Tenth Problem was one of the twenty-three mathematical problems posed to the international mathematical community by famed German mathematician **David Hilbert** (1862–1943; see biography in this chapter) in 1900. The Tenth Problem had stumped mathematicians for decades and, before Robinson and her colleagues tackled it, was believed to be unsolvable. Robinson, who sought greater opportunities for women in mathematics (see essay The Emergence of Women in Mathematics in this chapter), was the first woman to serve as president of the American Mathematical Society.

Endures illnesses as a child

Robinson was born on December 8, 1919, in St. Louis, Missouri. When she was two years old, her mother died. Robinson's father took her and her older sister to live with their grandmother in the desert near Phoenix, Arizona. The girls were reunited with their father one year later, when he remarried and moved the family to Point Loma, California (near San Diego).

At age nine, Robinson caught scarlet fever. She was kept in isolation for one month during her illness and shortly thereafter came down with rheumatic fever, a more serious illness that sometimes occurs with scarlet fever. Again Robinson had to be quarantined, this time in the home of a nurse. After one year Robinson was well enough to return home, but she was still so weak that she had to spend the next year in bed. She was tutored three times a week during that period. When Robinson recovered, she finished high school and took classes at San Diego State College. Her plan was to become a math teacher in a public school.

Seeks higher education in mathematics

Soon Robinson had gone beyond what her math teachers at San Diego State could teach her, and she sought a greater challenge. She transferred to the University of California at Berkeley, known for the strength of its mathematics program. After graduating with a bachelor's degree in 1940, Robinson began a graduate program and became a teaching assistant at Berkeley. One of Robinson's favorite classes, number theory, was taught by a professor named Raphael Robinson. The two found they had much in common, and in 1941 they married.

Because of rules barring both members of a married couple from serving on the faculty at Berkeley, Robinson had to give up her teaching fellowship. Around that time Robinson learned that, because of her childhood illnesses, she would not be able to have children. She sank into depression but was pulled out of it by her desire to pursue mathematics. She then entered a doctoral program at Berkeley and wrote her dissertation on number theory. Robinson received her Ph.D. in 1948.

Contributes to solution of Hilbert's Tenth Problem

Robinson next went to work at the Rand Corporation and later worked on a hydrodynamics (relating to the motion of fluids) project at Stanford University. In 1976 she became a full professor of mathematics at Berkeley.

Julia Bowman Robinson. (Reproduced by permission of Mathematisches Forschunginstitut Oberwolfach.)

Throughout her career, Robinson investigated a number of mathematical problems and published several papers. She spent decades trying to conquer Hilbert's Tenth Problem: how to solve a Diophantine equation (a polynomial [consisting of several terms] equation with several variables) using only integers (positive or negative whole numbers).

Robinson had figured out many aspects of the problem but could not complete the solution. The final part of the answer came in 1970, when a young Russian mathematician named Yuri Matijasevich constructed the missing part of the solution using a simple number series. Robinson visited the Soviet Union in 1971 to work with Matijasevich. Both mathematicians received tremendous acclaim for their joint solution of Hilbert's Tenth Problem.

Becomes president of American Mathematical Society

Despite her ongoing health problems, Robinson enjoyed a busy and varied career as a mathematician. In 1975 she became the first female mathematician elected to the National Academy of Sciences and in 1980 became only the second woman to present the American Mathematical Society (AMS) Colloquium Lecture. She began serving as an officer of the AMS in 1978, and in 1982 Robinson was selected to be the body's first female president.

In the summer of 1984, while presiding over the summer meeting of the AMS, Robinson learned she had leukemia. She died of the disease one year later, on July 30, 1985.

ALAN M. TURING (1912–1954)
British mathematician

Alan Turing was a mathematical visionary who theorized about programmable computers years before the first one was developed. Turing put his ideas about programming to work during World War II (1939–45), when he oversaw the development of a machine that could crack the codes used by the German military. His work played an important part in figuring out the German codes, an accomplishment that was critical in the victory of the Allies (the United States, Great Britain, France, and the Soviet Union). He spent the latter part of his career exploring fundamental questions on the nature of intelligence and its artificial creation.

A lonely childhood

Turing was born on June 23, 1912, in London, England, the second son of Ethel Sara Stoney and Julius Mathison Turing. Turing's parents lived much of the time in India, then a British colony, where Julius Turing was a high official in the British civil service. Turing's mother felt that India was an unsuitable place to raise children, so she left her sons in the care of relatives in England. Turing was lonely as a child, and his feelings of isolation increased when he was sent to an elite boarding school at the age of thirteen. There he fell in love with another boy (although he kept his feelings secret) and became depressed when the boy developed tuberculosis—then a fatal lung disease—and died in 1930.

Turing was an inconsistent student who excelled at mathematics and organic chemistry but had little interest in other subjects. His homework was sloppy and riddled with mistakes, and he refused to do assignments that he did not consider important. However, he made up for his classroom shortcomings by scoring well on year-end exams.

Envisions Turing machine

After finishing high school, Turing won a scholarship to King's College at Cambridge University and enrolled in 1931. In college, he became fascinated with problems of mathematical logic and distinguished himself as an outstanding thinker. After graduation, in 1935 Turing was elected a fellow of the college (a position usually reserved for older graduates) that gave him a yearly stipend.

Turing next went to Princeton University in New Jersey for graduate studies. There he encountered some of the greatest mathematical minds of all times, including Hungarian-American computer scientist John von Neumann (1903–1957; see box on page 130) and German-American physicist Albert Einstein (1879–1955). In 1936 Turing made his most lasting contribution to mathematics: he published a paper called "On Computable Numbers," in which he described a theoretical computer—which came to be called a "Turing machine"—that operated according to a set of instructions. The instructions were encoded as a grid of black and white squares on a long strip of paper. Turing concluded that a computer could solve any mathematical problem, regardless of its complexity, by following a series of simple steps. At a time when computers did not yet exist, Turing essentially provided a blueprint for the modern digital computer.

Alan Turing. (Reproduced by permission of Photo Researchers, Inc.)

A *Time* magazine article of March 29, 1999, put Turing's machine in historical context as follows: "So many ideas and technological advances converged to create the modern computer that it is foolhardy to give one person the credit for inventing it. But the fact remains that everyone who taps at a keyboard, opening a spreadsheet or a word-processing program, is working on an incarnation of a Turing machine."

Helps crack German military codes

Just after the outbreak of World War II, the British government recruited Turing to join a secret team working to crack the military code created by the Germans' Enigma machine. By making changes to the Enigma, the

Germans could continually increase the complexity of their code, thus remaining one step ahead of the British. Turing was a leader of the group of mathematicians and engineers that created Colossus, widely considered to be the first electronic computer. Using Colossus, Turing's group broke the code the German military used to communicate with U-boats (submarines) in the North Atlantic and provided the Allied forces with intelligence that helped them win the war.

Theorizes about artificial intelligence

After the war, Turing worked for a short time at the National Physical Laboratory in London. He then became deputy director of the Royal Society Computing Laboratory at Manchester University. There he began to research the nature of intelligence and explore how a machine could be made to think—a field that today is called artificial intelligence. In 1950 Turing published a landmark paper, "Computing Machinery and Intelligence," in which he predicted that within fifty years computers would be designed that could copy the human process of thinking. Such a computer, he wrote, would be able to play chess, learn and translate languages, and perform mathematical functions.

Life takes tragic turn

In 1952, a tragic chain of events began that led to Turing's death. After his house was burglarized, Turing admitted to police that he had been romantically involved with a man who may have known the burglar. Homosexuality in England was a felony at that time, and as a result Turing was tried and convicted of "gross indecency." As an alternative to prison, Turing chose to undergo hormone treatments designed to diminish his sex drive. The injection of female hormones caused undesirable changes in his body, and the publicity surrounding the affair was a source of great embarrassment for him. On June 7, 1954, Turing died after swallowing cyanide. Although there is some question as to whether it was an accident, his death was officially ruled a suicide.

◻ HERMANN WEYL (1885–1955)

German-American mathematician

Hermann Weyl was one of the greatest mathematicians of his generation. He made his mark on a range of mathematical disciplines, from the philosophy of mathematics and the theory of relativity to quantum mechanics (physical principles used to describe submicroscopic phenomena). Weyl was considered unusual among mathematicians for his love of poetry and his tendency to sprinkle lines from poems throughout dry mathematical papers. After spending the bulk of his career in Germany, Weyl, along with many other German mathematicians, fled to the United States to escape the Nazis (see essay The Devastation of Mathematics in Hitler's Germany).

Childhood and education

Weyl was born on November 9, 1885, in a small town outside Hamburg, Germany. His mother had inherited money, which allowed him to go to top-notch schools. Weyl attended the Gymnasium at Altona during middle and high school years. (In Germany, a gymnasium is a classical preparatory school for college-bound students.) There, his high intelligence came to the attention of the headmaster, who was related to the famed mathematician **David Hilbert** (1862–1943; see biography in this chapter). The headmaster helped get Weyl a place among Hilbert's students at the University of Göttingen.

Weyl attended the university for five years, receiving his doctorate in 1908—with Hilbert as his advisor. Weyl remained at Göttingen for the next few years as an instructor.

Explores variety of mathematical topics

In 1913 Weyl took a position at the National Technical University in Zurich, Switzerland. That same year he married a woman named Helene Joseph; in the coming years the couple had two sons.

Some of Weyl's most important work was done early in his career in Zurich. He concentrated mainly on theoretical pursuits, such as his groundbreaking work on the properties and distribution of irrational numbers (numbers, such as the square root of a negative, which cannot be expressed as a ratio of two whole numbers). Weyl also worked in the areas of geometry and topology (the study of properties of geometric forms that remain constant even when exposed to certain forces, such as stretching or bending). When World War I (1914–18) broke out, Weyl served briefly in the German army.

Hermann Weyl. (Reproduced by permission of AP/Wide World Photos.)

After the war, Weyl spent one year working with German-born American physicist Albert Einstein (1879–1955) on the latter's theory of general relativity, a theory stating that gravity is a result of curved space-time (a four-dimensional construct that unites the three dimensions of space with time). Specifically, Weyl ironed out some of the mathematical basis of Einstein's theory. He also wrote a book titled *Space, Time, Matter* (German-language edition published in 1918) that explained relativity in nontechnical language.

Questions mathematical underpinnings

One of Weyl's main undertakings in the 1920s was examining the philosophical basis of mathematics. His research caused him to clash with his former mentor, Hilbert, a defender of "classical" mathematics. The classical, or formal, method claimed that any mathematical statement fell into one of two categories: true or not true. Weyl was attracted to the ideas of Dutch mathematician Luitzen Egbertus Jan Brouwer (1881–1966), who championed an "intuitive" approach that added an "unproven" category to the first two. Weyl ultimately began to distrust the intuitive approach, rather pointing out the pros and cons of both schools.

Leaves Nazi Germany

In 1930, after Hilbert retired, Weyl took over as chair of Göttingen's mathematics department. His time at the famous university, however, did not last long. Weyl despaired at Adolf Hitler (1889–1945) and his National Socialist (Nazi) Party's campaign to force Jews out of German universities. Although not a Jew himself, Weyl decided to leave as well because he was concerned about harassment due to his wife's Jewish heritage; he also left in general protest of the Nazi policies.

"I could not bear to live under the rule of that demon [Hitler]," Weyl wrote in his memoirs, "who had dishonored the name of Germany, and although the wrench was hard and the mental agony so cruel that I suffered a severe breakdown, I shook the dust of the fatherland from my feet."

Weyl came to the United States to take a faculty position at the Institute for Advanced Study at Princeton University. There he again worked briefly with Einstein and was seen as a link between the world's old mathematical center at Göttingen and the new one in the United States. Weyl became an American citizen, but after World War II (1939–45) ended he divided his time between the United States and Zurich. He died in Zurich on December 8, 1955, one month after his seventieth birthday.

ANDREW WILES (1953–)

British mathematician

Andrew Wiles is the most celebrated living mathematician. He achieved instant celebrity status in 1993 for his proof of history's most famous unsolved mathematical problem: Fermat's last theorem. The theorem, written by French mathematician Pierre Fermat (1601–1665), expanded on the Pythagorean theorem for finding the lengths of the sides of a right triangle and set limits for that equation. A proof of Fermat's last theorem had stumped mathematicians for more than three centuries before Wiles's shocking announcement.

Boyhood interest in mathematics

Wiles was born April 11, 1953, in Cambridge, England, the son of an Oxford University religion professor. Although he did not show a great gift for math as a child, he was intrigued by Fermat's last theorem—which he had first read about in his local library at age ten. "It looked so simple," Wiles stated in an interview with NOVA Online, "and yet all the great mathematicians in history couldn't solve it. Here was a problem that a ten-year-old could understand, and I knew from that moment that I would never let it go." As a teenager, and later as a college student, Wiles spent countless hours trying to prove the theorem.

Begins career at Princeton

Wiles went to Oxford University as an undergraduate, earning his bachelor's degree in 1974. He then went to Cambridge University, completing his master's degree in 1977 and his Ph.D. in 1980. The following year Wiles traveled to the United States to conduct research at Princeton University's Institute for Advanced Study.

In 1982 Wiles was named a professor of mathematics at Princeton. For a time, he put Fermat's last theorem on the back burner in order to concentrate on his work responsibilities. He did, however, keep an eye on developments in the math world that might shed some light on the solution.

Andrew Wiles.
(Reproduced by permission of Photo Researchers, Inc.)

Interest rekindled in Fermat's last theorem

In 1986, American mathematician Ken Ribet provided a missing piece to the Fermat puzzle by showing that the Taniyama-Shimura conjecture (named for the two Japanese mathematicians who wrote it in the 1950s; a "conjecture" is a fascinating but unproven theory) was linked to Fermat's last theorem. The Taniyama-Shimura conjecture suggested an association between elliptical curves and certain equations. Ribet argued that if the Taniyama-Shimura conjecture could be proved, then it would logically follow that Fermat's last theorem could also be proved.

Fermat's Last Theorem

Fermat's last theorem begins with the Pythagorean theorem (named after Greek mathematician Pythagoras [c. 580–c. 500 B.C.E.]), which states that $x^2 + y^2 = z^2$, and describes how the lengths of sides in a right triangle are related to one another. It states that the square of the longest side is equal to the sum of the squares of the other two sides. Fermat theorized that if each side were cubed, instead of squared, or raised to an even higher power, then x, y, and z could not all be whole numbers. (For example, 33 + 43 = 91, but the cube root of 91 is not a whole number.) In sum, he wrote that there are no whole-number solutions to the problem $x^n + y^n = z^n$, where n is greater than two.

Fermat had scribbled his theorem in the margin of a Greek book on mathematics, along with the note: "I have discovered a truly remarkable proof but this margin is too small to contain it." There is no record of Fermat ever having provided the proof elsewhere, and, in fact, many modern mathematicians doubt that he actually had one. (A proof, in the mathematical sense, is a line of reasoning consisting of many steps.)

At the end of 1986, Wiles decided it was time to once again focus on Fermat's last theorem. In an interview with NOVA Online, Wiles described what he felt when he heard about Ribet's accomplishment. "I knew that moment that the course of my life was changing," he said, "because this meant that to prove Fermat's last theorem all I had to do was to prove the Taniyama-Shimura conjecture." For the next seven years Wiles secretly worked on the proof. Secrecy is rare in mathematics, where scholars frequently work together, but his colleagues believed he was only involved in research on the Taniyama-Shimura conjecture.

Shares his proof with the world

In the summer of 1993, Wiles was satisfied that he had solved the famous theorem. He chose to share his work with the world at a conference at the Isaac Newton Institute at Cambridge University. Without revealing his plan ahead of time, Wiles signed up to give a series of three lectures. Because

Wiles had been out of circulation for so long, and rumors had been circulating that Wiles had a big announcement to make; his lectures drew a big crowd. He did not even mention Fermat until his third lecture, but as it became apparent that he was closing in on a proof of Fermat's theorem, the excitement at the conference grew. When Wiles finished delivering his 200-page proof, his accomplishment made headlines around the world.

Once mathematicians had a chance to examine Wiles's proof, however, they discovered an error in a critical portion. Although at first the error seemed minor, it turned out to be much more significant than anyone had thought. Only after a year of work by Wiles and one of his former students, Richard Taylor, was it finally resolved and the proof accepted.

After his once-in-a-lifetime mathematical conquest, Wiles returned to his teaching and research duties at Princeton. Because of his famous proof, he has won many prizes and honors.

BRIEF BIOGRAPHIES ◣

◣ DAVID BLACKWELL (1919–)

American theoretical statistician (a mathematician specializing in theories about statistics; see essay Advances in the Field of Statistics in this chapter) who was the seventh African American to earn a Ph.D. in mathematics (in 1941, at the University of Illinois). (See essay The Emergence of African Americans in Mathematics in this chapter.) He was also the first, and so far only, African American mathematician to be elected to the National Academy of Sciences. Blackwell made important contributions to Bayesian statistical analysis (a method of including observed data in estimates of probability, named after English mathematician Thomas Bayes [1702–1761]), dynamic programming (a system of mathematical reasoning that analyzes decision-making processes by starting with the best possible outcome and working backwards), and game theory (a branch of mathematics concerned with the analysis of conflict situations; see essay The Development of Game Theory in this chapter). After teaching at Howard University, Blackwell served as chair of the statistics department at the University of California, Berkeley.

◣ FÉLIX-ÉDOUARD-JUSTIN-ÉMILE BOREL (1871–1956)

French mathematician noted for his work on complex numbers (a combination of real and imaginary numbers, such as the square roots of negative numbers) and development of methods for measuring complicated two-dimensional surfaces. Borel also wrote *Space and Time* in 1922 to explain

Albert Einstein's (1879–1955) theory of relativity (a theory stating that gravity is a result of curved space-time, a four-dimensional construct that unites the three dimensions of space with time) to a general audience. He was active in French politics and helped shape the country's policies regarding science and math education and research.

⚠ LUITZEN EGBERTUS JAN BROUWER (1881–1966)

Dutch mathematician who focused on two branches of mathematics: topology (the study of properties of geometric forms that remain constant even when exposed to certain forces, such as stretching or bending) and logic. His most lasting contribution was his fixed-point theorem, which stated that for any change affecting all points on a circle, at least one point must remain unchanged. Brouwer also questioned the basis of mathematical proofs, suggesting that in addition to the categories "true" and "not true," there should be a third category: "unproven." His intuitionist school of thought (as it was called) held that mathematical truths are a matter of common sense.

⚠ ALONZO CHURCH (1903–1995)

American mathematician who, with his more famous student **Alan M. Turing** (1912–1954; see biography in this chapter), helped develop the foundations of computer science. Church created a key principle of computer logic: the repetition of simple operations in order to solve complex problems. He also authored Church's theorem, which states that there is no method to guarantee that one will always arrive at the correct conclusions in mathematics. Church taught at Princeton University for nearly four decades, during which time he trained many students who went on to make important contributions to mathematics.

⚠ PAUL JOSEPH COHEN (1934–)

American mathematician who solved the first of the twenty-three problems posed to the Second International Congress of Mathematics by German mathematician **David Hilbert** (1862–1943; see biography in this chapter) in 1900. Cohen's solution, for which he received the Fields Medal—the highest honor in mathematics—in 1966, involved his discovery that the continuum hypothesis (a hypothesis regarding different sizes of infinite sets; it asks the question of whether there is an infinite set whose size is bigger than the infinity of whole numbers but smaller than the infinity of real numbers) is independent of set theory (a field of mathematics dealing with operations on sets of numbers grouped by their characteristics and properties). In other words, Cohen found that Hilbert's first question is unanswerable. Cohen has taught mathematics at Stanford University since 1961.

▲ SIMON KIRWAN DONALDSON (1957–)

English mathematician who advanced the field of topology, the study of properties of geometric forms that remain constant even when exposed to certain forces, such as stretching or bending. Donaldson won the 1986 Fields Medal (mathematics' highest honor) for his work on defining four-dimensional (length, width, height, and time) space. His work has been useful in theoretical mathematics as well as applied mathematics, which are mathematics used to solve practical problems in science, engineering, and economics. Donaldson is on the mathematics faculties of both Oxford University in England and Stanford University in California.

▲ ETTA ZUBER FALCONER (1933–)

American mathematician who was the tenth African American woman to earn a Ph.D. in the field, from Emory University in 1969 (see essay The Emergence of African Americans in Mathematics in this chapter). She also holds a master's degree in computer science from Atlanta University. Falconer has been celebrated for her work in group theory concerning the symmetries (the correspondence of parts on opposite sides of an entity, as in the arms and legs of human beings) of objects and of space itself. She served as chair of the mathematics department at Spelman College in Atlanta from 1971 to 1985 and won the Louise Hay Award for her outstanding achievements in mathematics education in 1995.

Etta Falconer.
(Reproduced by permission of Ms. Etta Falconer.)

▲ KURT FRIEDRICH GÖDEL (1906–1978)

Austrian-American mathematician whose name has become linked with the incompleteness theorem. That theorem states that within any axiomatic system (one containing universally accepted principles or rules, known as axioms), there are propositions that cannot be proved or disproved using the axioms of that system. In other words, Gödel demonstrated that at the heart of mathematics are statements that are clearly true but cannot be proved by axioms. His theorem upset mathematicians' long-held assumption that their field was supported by absolute truths. Gödel moved to the United States in 1933 and accepted a position at the Institute for Advanced Study at Princeton University. Later in his career he concentrated on philosophical questions. Gödel developed an extreme fear of food poisoning as he aged, and he died of malnutrition in 1978.

▲ ALEXANDRE GROTHENDIECK (1928–)

German-French mathematician who conducted highly theoretical work on algebraic geometry (a field that combines geometric shapes with algebraic equations) and contributed to mathematical logic. Much of Grothendieck's work was so complex that it was beyond the grasp of all but the most advanced mathematicians. He won the Swedish Academy's Crafoord Prize for his accomplishments in 1988, but he rejected it due to what he described as growing dishonesty and ambition among mathematicians and scientists. Grothendieck is a devoted pacifist (a person who opposes war) and environmentalist who has long pushed for military disarmament and pesticide-free farming.

▲ THOMAS C. HALES (1958–)

American mathematician and University of Michigan professor who gained worldwide fame in the summer of 1998 for his proof of Kepler's sphere-packing conjecture. That conjecture (a fascinating but unproven theory) had been proposed by German astronomer Johannes Kepler (1571–1630) in 1611; it stated that the most efficient way to pack spheres of equal size is in staggered layers, so that the spheres in each layer occupy the hollows made by the spheres in the layer below. Until Hales, no mathematician had been able to prove Kepler's conjecture. In 1999, Hales again made headlines with his proof of another packing question: the hexagonal honeycomb conjecture. That conjecture holds that hexagons are the most efficient way to enclose many unit areas in a plane.

▲ LOUISE SCHMIR HAY (1935–1989)

Polish-American mathematician who earned an international reputation for her accomplishments in mathematical logic and theoretical computer science. Hay helped found the Association of Women in Mathematics (AWM) in 1971 (see essay The Emergence of Women in Mathematics in this chapter). In 1980, when she accepted the chair of the mathematics department at the University of Illinois in Chicago, she became the first woman to hold such a position at a major American research university. After Hay's death from cancer in 1989, the AWM honored her by establishing the Louise Hay Award for Contributions to Mathematics Education.

◢ KUNIHIKO KODAIRA (1915–1997)

Japanese mathematician and theoretical physicist who conducted ground-breaking research in a variety of mathematical areas and had a distinguished university career both in Japan (at the University of Tokyo) and in the United States (at Princeton's Institute for Advanced Study, Harvard, Johns Hopkins, and Stanford). He conducted much of his early research while isolated from the world's mathematical centers in the United States and Europe, because during World War II (1939-45) Japan was at war with those nations. In 1954 he became the first Japanese mathematician to receive the important Fields Medal. Kodaira wrote several mathematics textbooks used by Japanese students.

◢ ANDREI NIKOLAEVICH KOLMOGOROV (1903–1987)

Russian mathematician who made important contributions to almost every area of his subject and was best known as the founder of probability theory (a mathematical theory explaining how likely a given event is to occur). Kolmogorov was also noted for his scholarship in other fields, such as physics and linguistics (the scientific study of language). He spent most of his career as director of the institute of mathematics at Moscow State University. During the 1960s, as chair of the Commission for Mathematical Education for the Academy of Sciences, he helped shape the Soviet Union's mathematics education program.

◢ CHRISTINE LADD-FRANKLIN (1847–1930)

American mathematician who made important contributions to symbolic logic (the principles of reasoning as it regards to sets of symbols) and the optics of color vision. She attended graduate courses in mathematics at Johns Hopkins University at a time when the institution did not formally admit women and wrote a dissertation titled "The Algebra of Logic." Ladd-Franklin conducted research in the field of physiological optics (the study of the function of vision in living organisms) and color vision for more than three decades. She was finally awarded a Ph.D. from Johns Hopkins in 1926, forty-four years after she submitted her dissertation. Throughout her career, Ladd-Franklin pushed for equal opportunities for women in education and academics (see essay The Emergence of Women in Mathematics in this chapter).

◢ BENOIT B. MANDELBROT (1924–)

Polish-French mathematician who was one of the founders of fractal geometry. (Fractals are shapes that maintain similar properties and relationships at all levels of magnification. Furthermore, each component part of the fractal, when magnified, resembles the structure as a whole.) Fractal concepts have seen widespread application in areas such as astronomy (particularly in studying how galaxies form), cellular processes, and computer animation. Mandelbrot has taught and conducted research not only in mathematics but also in engineering, physiology, and economics and has developed computer graphics programs to represent fractal concepts.

◸ HERMANN MINKOWSKI (1864–1909)

Russian-German mathematician who, during his relatively short career, made contributions to many fields of mathematics, including the mathematical basis of the theory of relativity. One of Minkowski's most important achievements was developing the geometry of numbers, which involves applying geometrical concepts to volume. His work had practical applications in packing efficiency (the best way to pack a space given objects of different shapes). In 1902 Minkowski joined the faculty of the University of Göttingen to work with his friend **David Hilbert** (1862–1943; see biography in this chapter); his most famous pupil was Albert Einstein (1879–1955). In 1909 Minkowski died suddenly of a burst appendix.

◸ RUTH MOUFANG (1905–1977)

German mathematician who helped create the algebraic analysis of projective planes, a discipline that combines geometry and algebra. She also published several papers about theoretical physics, many of which focused on elasticity theory (principles governing the relationship between a deforming force and the resulting change in shape or size of an object). Moufang received her Ph.D. from the University of Frankfurt in 1931; however, the Nazi government barred her from accepting a professorship due to her gender. Moufang sought employment elsewhere and became the first German woman with a doctorate to work in industry. In 1946, after the Nazi defeat in World War II (1939–45), Moufang joined the faculty of the University of Frankfurt.

Benoit Mandelbrot.
(Reproduced by
permission of Photo
Researchers, Inc.)

◸ KARL PEARSON (1857–1936)

British mathematician who became known as the father of statistics (see essay Advances in the Field of Statistics in this chapter). In the 1890s,

Pearson developed a mathematical method for testing the degree of correlation between different phenomena; in other words, determining the likelihood that if one phenomenon occurs, another phenomenon will also occur. An example of Pearson's test would be determining whether changes in height are linked to changes in weight.

SIR ROGER PENROSE (1931–)

English mathematician who worked with British physicist Stephen Hawking (1942–) to explain the theoretical basis of black holes (the remains of massive stars that have burned out their nuclear fuel and collapsed under the force of gravity into single points of infinite mass and density). As a professor at Cambridge, Penrose served on Hawking's dissertation committee, wrote books with Hawking, and received awards jointly with Hawking for the pair's work on black holes. Penrose provided a mathematical proof that the matter within a black hole must eventually collapse under gravity into a single point. His insights have shed light on the life cycles of stars, as well as on our understanding of the origin of the universe.

STEPHEN SMALE (1930–)

American mathematician who conducted research on topology (the study of properties of geometric forms that remain constant even when exposed to certain forces, such as stretching or bending), the mathematical theory of economics, computer science, dynamic systems (a mathematical description of the motion of systems acted upon by outside forces), and other areas. Throughout his career, both as a student (at the University of Michigan) and a professor (at the University of California, Berkeley), Smale was active in anti-war protests. In the 1980s, he focused mainly on computer science in the belief that computers have the potential to revolutionize mathematics (see essay The Development of Computational Mathematics in this chapter).

OLGA TAUSSKY-TODD (1906–1995)

Austrian-born American mathematician who conducted groundbreaking research on matrix theory (the study of sets of elements in a rectangular array, which are subject to operations such as addition or multiplication according to certain rules) and its application to emerging computer technology. Taussky-Todd was also noted for her work on number theory, which is the study of integers and their relationships. Taussky-Todd earned her Ph.D. in 1930 at the University of Vienna and then worked with German-born American mathematician **Emmy Amalie Noether** (1882–1935; see biography in this chapter) at the University of Göttengin in Germany. In 1933 Taussky-Todd, a Jewish woman, was forced out of her profession by the rise of the Nazi Party (see essay The Devastation of Mathematics in Hitler's Germany in this chapter). She left Germany and taught college in England and in the United States. In 1957 Taussky-Todd joined the faculty of the California Institute of Technology; she remained there until her retirement in 1977. Taussky-Todd published more than 200 papers throughout her career.

◮ RENÉ FRÉDÉRIC THOM (1923–)

French mathematician best known for developing catastrophe theory, the theory of dynamic (moving) systems in which slow growth is accompanied by major, or catastrophic, alterations in form. For example, if the load carried by a bridge is gradually increased, the bridge will slowly bend at a uniform rate until the load becomes too heavy, at which point it will suddenly collapse. Thom also made contributions to topology (the study of properties of geometric forms that remain constant even when exposed to certain forces, such as stretching or bending) and the philosophy of mathematics. He won the Fields Medal in 1958 for his pioneering work on cobordism, an attempt to describe, in noncalculus mathematical terms, those situations in which a gradual change in forces leads to an abrupt change (or catastrophe). In the latter part of his career, Thom turned his attention to optical problems in physics and embryology (the study of early development in living things).

Olga Taussky-Todd.
(Reproduced by permission of Ms. Olga Taussky-Todd.)

◮ ANDRÉ WEIL (1906–1998)

French mathematician who advanced algebraic geometry (a field that combines geometric shapes with algebraic equations), group theory (a theory concerning the symmetries [correspondence of parts on opposite sides of an entity, such as a person's arms and legs] of objects and of space itself), number theory (the study of integers and their relationships), and other areas. His theory of "uniform space," a highly theoretical mathematical construct, was hailed as a major discovery. Weil was teaching at the University of Strasbourg in France when World War II (1939–45) broke out; he fled to the United States in advance of Nazi Germany's invasion of his country. After holding several teaching positions in the United States and Brazil, Weil taught at the University of Chicago from 1947 to 1958 and then at Princeton's Institute for Advanced Study until his retirement in 1976.

◤ GRACE EMILY CHISHOLM YOUNG (1868–1944)

British mathematician and the first woman to receive a Ph.D. (in 1895) from a German university in any field. Young attended the German University of Göttengin because English universities did not yet admit women (see essay The Emergence of Women in Mathematics in this chapter). With her husband, fellow mathematician William Young, she wrote a well-received textbook on set theory (a theory concerning operations on sets of numbers grouped by their characteristics and properties); she also wrote a popular textbook on geometry. Young combined her mathematical research with raising six children (often on her own, as her husband worked overseas), including several published papers on the foundations of calculus. Later in life Young abandoned mathematics in favor of studying language, medicine, music, and literature, and she became an author of children's fiction.

RESEARCH AND ACTIVITY IDEAS

1. New Math, a method of teaching mathematics that emphasized the conceptual (intuitive) understanding of the foundations of mathematics over the memorization of facts and formulas, began to be used in American public schools in the 1960s. In the 1990s, another new type of math education, typically called standards math, was adopted. That method emphasized teamwork, the use of three-dimensional objects, and problem solving in real-life situations. Like the 1960s experiment, standards math has been the center of a heated debate. Outline the arguments of those who support and those who oppose standards math.

2. One of the best-known examples of game theory is the prisoners' dilemma. This game involves a scenario in which two suspects in a bank robbery are interviewed separately. If both keep quiet, they will each get one year in jail on weapons charges. If both confess and accuse the other, they will each get sentenced to ten years in prison. If one agrees to testify against the other, who keeps quiet, the cooperative one goes free and the other one goes to jail for twenty years. Conduct research to learn about the paradoxes in the prisoners' dilemma and how it can be applied to real-world circumstances. Then pose the problem to your classmates, and record and analyze their responses.

3. Write about the historical conditions (in particular, segregation laws) that have made it harder for African Americans to participate in

higher education and pursue careers in mathematics. What were the factors that caused those conditions to change? What are some current challenges facing African Americans in the area of mathematics education?

(4) In 1933, when dictator Adolf Hitler (1889–1945) came to power in Germany, his National Socialist (Nazi) Party created a series of laws that restricted the activities of Jewish people, finally ending in their mass slaughter during World War II (1939–45). One of the Nazis' earliest moves was to fire Jewish instructors from German universities. The result was a "brain drain" of Jewish intellectuals and their sympathetic colleagues from Germany; many of them emigrated to the United States. Create a time line of policies and practices in Nazi Germany that destroyed Germany's position as world leader in mathematics.

(5) Many of the world's leading mathematicians and scientists, particularly those who left Europe during World War II (1939–45), spent some portion of their careers at Princeton University's Institute for Advanced Study (IAS). Research the history of the IAS. What famous intellectuals helped shape the institute and what drew them there? What were some of the projects that took place at the IAS?

(6) The Association for Women in Mathematics (AWM) is a nonprofit organization founded in 1971 to support women in the mathematical sciences. Take a look at the AWM Web site (http://www.awm-math.org/) and write about the organization's history, services, and present-day activities.

FOR MORE INFORMATION

Books

Albers, Donald J., and G. L. Alexanderson, eds. *Mathematical People: Profiles and Interviews.* Cambridge, MA: Birkhauser Boston, 1985.

Beasley, John D. *The Mathematics of Games.* New York: Oxford University Press, 1989.

Billings, Charlene W. *Supercomputers: Shaping the Future.* New York: Facts on File, Inc., 1995.

Bunch, Bryan, and Alexander Hellemans. *The Timetables of Technology: A Chronology of the Most Important People and Events in the History of Technology.* New York: Simon and Schuster, 1993.

Computer Age. Alexandria, VA: Time-Life Books, 1992.

Cooney, Miriam P., ed. *Celebrating Women in Mathematics and Science.* Reston, VA: National Council of Teachers of Mathematics, 1996.

Davis, Morton D. *Game Theory.* New York: Basic Books, Inc., 1970.

Haber, Louis. *Black Pioneers of Science and Invention.* San Diego: Harcourt Brace & Company, 1970.

Henderson, Harry. *Modern Mathematicians.* New York: Facts on File, Inc., 1996: pp. 58–69.

Hill, John. *Exploring Information Technology.* Austin, TX: Raintree Steck-Vaughn, 1993.

McGrayne, Sharon Bertsch. *Nobel Prize Women in Science: Their Lives, Struggles, and Momentous Discoveries.* New York: Carol Publishing Group, 1993.

Morrow, Charlene, and Teri Perl, eds. *Notable Women in Mathematics.* Westport, CT: Greenwood Press, 1998.

Moses, Robert P., and Charles E. Cobb Jr. *Radical Equations: Math Literacy and Civil Rights.* Boston: Beacon Press, 2001.

Nardo, Don, ed. *The Rise of Nazi Germany.* San Diego, CA: Greenhaven Press, Inc., 1999.

Osen, Lynn M. *Women in Mathematics.* Cambridge, MA: The MIT Press, 1974.

Reid, Constance. *Hilbert.* New York: Springer-Verlag, 1970.

Riedel, Manfred G. *Winning With Numbers: A Kid's Guide to Statistics.* Englewood Cliffs, NJ: Prentice-Hall, 1978.

Schechter, Bruce. *My Brain Is Open: The Mathematical Journeys of Paul Erdös.* New York: Simon & Schuster, 1998.

Sertima, Ivan Van. *Blacks in Science: Ancient and Modern.* New Brunswick, NJ: Transaction Books, 1983.

Smoothey, Marion. *Let's Investigate Statistics.* New York: Marshall Cavendish, 1993.

Srivastava, Jane Jonas. *Statistics (A Young Math Book).* New York: Thomas Y. Crowell Company, 1973.

Stern, Fritz. *Einstein's German World.* Princeton, NJ: Princeton University Press, 1999.

Stewart, Gail B. *Hitler's Reich.* San Diego, CA: Lucent Books, 1994.

Vajda, Steven. *Mathematical Games and How to Play Them.* New York: Ellis Horwood, 1992.

Williamson, David. *The Third Reich.* New York: The Bookwright Press, 1989.

Periodicals

Argetsinger, Amy. "Black Women Beginning to Count in Mathematics." *The Washington Post.* December 22, 2000: p. B01.

Folger, Tim. "Sure, Pierre. Sure You Knew." *Discover.* January 1994: p. 61.

Gray, Paul. "Computer Scientist: Alan Turing. While Addressing a Problem in the Arcane Field of Mathematical Logic, He Imagined a Machine That Could Mimic Human Reasoning. Sound Familiar?" *Time.* March 29, 1999: pp. 147+.

Heppenheimer, T. A. "How Von Neumann Showed the Way." *American Heritage of Invention & Technology.* Fall 1990: pp. 8–16.

Kronholz, June. "Numbers Racket: 'Standards' Math Is Creating a Big Division in Education Circles—It Favors Strategic Thinking, and a Good Guess Is OK, But Critics Call It Fuzzy—Multiplication Table as a Relic." *The Wall Street Journal.* November 5, 1997: p. A1.

Lemonick, Michael D. "Paul Erdös: The Oddball's Oddball." *Time.* March 29, 1999: p. 134.

Ohanian, Susan. "The New New Math." *Parents.* October 1995: p. 10.

Sheppard, Robert. "The New New Math." *Maclean's.* August 17, 1998: p. 48.

Whitmire, Richard. "Critics Say the Latest Math Methods Do Not Compute." *USA Today.* November 24, 1997: p. D5.

Zernike, Kate. "Test Results from States Reveal Gaps in Learning." *The New York Times.* April 9, 2000: p. A14.

Web sites

Agnes Scott College. *Biographies of Women Mathematicians.* http://www.agnesscott.edu/Lriddle/women/resource.htm (accessed March 21, 2002).

Association for Women in Mathematics. http://www.awm-math.org/ (accessed March 21, 2002).

"Hermann Weyl." *Museum of Tolerance Online Multimedia Learning Center.* http://www.wiesenthal.com/mot (accessed March 21, 2002).

Mathematics Enrichment Club. http://plus.maths.org/issue3/dynamic/ (accessed March 21, 2002).

"In Memoriam: Paul Erdös." *University of Chicago.* http://theory.cs.uchicago.edu/erdos.html (accessed March 21, 2002).

"Solving Fermat: Andrew Wiles." *NOVA Online.* http://www.pbs.org/wgbh/nova/proof/wiles.html (accessed March 21, 2002).

Williams, Scott W. *Mathematicians of the African Diaspora.* State University of New York at Buffalo. http://www.math.buffalo.edu/mad/mad0.html (accessed March 21, 2002).

chapter three Medicine

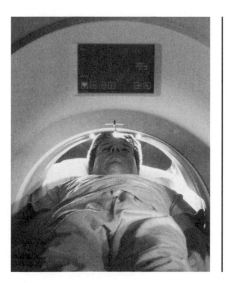

CHRONOLOGY

1912 Polish biochemist Casimir Funk isolates the substance in rice hulls that prevents beriberi and calls it "vitamine," later shortening the word to "vitamin."

1932 Hungarian-American biochemist Albert Szent-Györgyi identifies vitamin C as the substance that prevents the disease scurvy; in 1937 he wins the Nobel Prize in physiology or medicine for his achievement.

1932 German bacteriologist Gerhard Domagk isolates the first sulfa drug, which he calls Prontosil, for treating bacterial ailments in humans.

1940 Australian-English pathologist Howard Florey and German biochemist Ernst Chain purify penicillin for human use.

1948 The United Nations creates the World Health Organization (WHO), an international public health agency, with the goal of achieving for all peoples "the highest possible level of health."

1954 The first successful kidney transplant takes place in Boston, Massachusetts, from one identical twin to the other.

1954 American physician Jonas Salk develops the first vaccine for polio.

1960 The Food and Drug Administration (FDA) approves for use the birth control pill, which is the first safe, easily used, and reliable contraceptive.

1963 American surgeon Thomas Starzl performs the world's first successful human liver transplant.

1964 Surgeon General Luther Terry conclusively links cigarettes and other tobacco products to lung cancer in a landmark report titled *Smoking and Health: Report of the Advisory Committee to the Surgeon General of the Public Health Service.*

1967 South African surgeon Christiaan Barnard performs the world's first human heart transplant.

1981 The U.S. Centers for Disease Control (CDC) officially recognizes acquired immunodeficiency syndrome (AIDS) as a disease.

1984 American researcher Robert Gallo and French virologist Luc Montagnier discover the human immunodeficiency virus (HIV), the retrovirus that causes AIDS. Gallo develops a blood test that can detect the presence of HIV.

1997 The U.S. Food and Drug Administration (FDA) wins the right to regulate cigarettes and smokeless tobacco products (such as chewing tobacco) as "drug delivery devices."

2000 The FDA approves RU-486, the French abortion pill, for use in the United States. RU-486 provides a nonsurgical way to end a pregnancy before the seventh week after conception.

Background: A century of rapid progress

The field of medicine saw more progress during the twentieth century than it had during all of the previous two thousand years. The pace of medical advances was greatest in the decades after World War II (1939–45). During the twentieth century, many of the worst infectious diseases were controlled by vaccines, antibiotics, and improvements in sanitation and food safety. The campaign to vaccinate people against smallpox in the 1970s resulted in smallpox being virtually wiped out around the world—one of the greatest medical accomplishments of the century.

In the United States, the widespread use of vaccines and antibiotics meant that public health problems shifted from infectious, rapidly spreading illnesses to non-infectious conditions such as heart disease, cancer, and stroke. In poorer nations, however, large numbers of people continued to die from treatable or preventable diseases such as dysentery and malaria. Acquired immunodeficiency syndrome (AIDS), a fatal disease first diagnosed in the United States in the early 1980s, reached alarming levels worldwide in the 1990s. By the end of the century, AIDS had created severe health-care crises in many African nations.

A major shift in twentieth-century medicine in the United States was a growing reliance on complicated and expensive procedures and equipment. Organ transplants, magnetic resonance imaging (MRI) scanning, and AIDS drugs are three examples of medical triumphs that unfortunately have driven medical expenses sky-high. One result of this shift is that the price of even basic health-care services has risen so much that millions of Americans who do not have medical insurance can no longer afford them. This trend also widened the gulf between the types of treatments available in industrialized nations and developing nations and increased the difference in life expectancies between these two types of nations.

Public health efforts

Public health agencies in the United States and throughout the world made much progress during the twentieth century. Water treatment, particularly in industrialized nations, decreased the risk of diseases that are spread by water, such as typhoid and cholera. In some less-developed

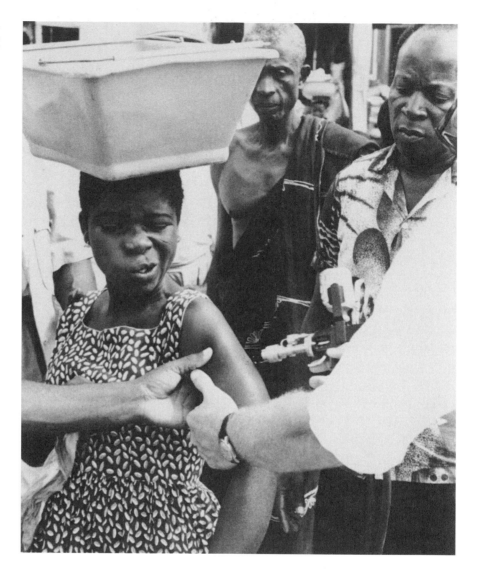

Young Nigerian girl winces as she receives a smallpox vaccination. The campaign to vaccinate people against smallpox in the 1970s resulted in the disease being virtually wiped out around the world. (Reproduced by permission of the Corbis Corporation.)

nations, however, where many people still drink untreated water, those diseases remain a serious problem. Another twentieth-century accomplishment was the development of vaccines for several nonbacterial infectious diseases, such as smallpox, polio, diphtheria, rabies, measles, cholera, and chicken pox. By the end of the twentieth century, 80 percent of the world's children had been vaccinated against major childhood diseases, and child mortality rates dropped sharply as a result.

Most industrialized nations and many developing nations have public health agencies that research and analyze health trends and carry out programs to protect and improve public health. On an international level, the

World Health Organization (WHO), founded by the United Nations (UN) in 1948, conducted vaccination and health education campaigns in developing nations that decreased the rates of both endemic (normally occurring in a population at a relatively constant rate) and epidemic (showing a rapid increase in the rate of infection) diseases.

Value of vitamins discovered

During the early twentieth century, scientific researchers determined the role vitamins play in fighting disease and maintaining health. These discoveries showed the importance of good nutrition in staying healthy. In the latter half of the 1900s, pellagra, beriberi, scurvy, and other diseases caused by vitamin deficiencies almost disappeared in the United States and other industrialized nations. In poor countries, however, large numbers of people continued to suffer from those conditions.

Researchers made tremendous progress in the 1920s and 1930s in identifying specific vitamins and understanding the role vitamins play in maintaining health. They discovered that vitamin D prevents rickets (a disease that weakens bones and particularly affects children); niacin prevents and cures pellagra (a disease that causes severe skin problems and diarrhea); thiamine prevents beriberi (a disease that causes nerve and gastrointestinal disorders); vitamin C keeps the skin, bones, teeth, and muscles healthy; and vitamin K promotes blood clotting. By 1950, vitamin pills were commercially available, with special formulas for children, adults, and pregnant women. Manufacturers also began adding vitamins to cereals, grains, flour, bread, and milk.

Antibiotics: powerful disease-fighting tools

The development of antibiotics, drugs that fight infections caused by bacteria, has changed the way we treat disease around the world. Antibiotics, which first became widely available during World War II, can cure pneumonia, tuberculosis, strep throat, scarlet fever, staph infection, venereal disease, spinal meningitis, and typhoid fever. Previously, people who suffered from these kinds of bacterial infections and illnesses had a high risk of dying. Because of their power to cure potentially fatal diseases, people saw antibiotics as miracle drugs.

However, the overuse and misuse of these drugs has created new strains of bacteria that are resistant to antibiotics. As a result, there are now some bacterial illnesses against which antibiotics are ineffective and for which there is no cure.

AIDS becomes a worldwide crisis

In the last few decades of the twentieth century, the AIDS crisis reached the level of a health emergency of worldwide proportions. While AIDS was first diagnosed in the United States in 1981, it spread rapidly to other continents.

By the year 2000, it had killed an estimated 22 million people worldwide. The hardest-hit continent was Africa, where 80 percent of all AIDS deaths occurred. At the beginning of the twenty-first century, about 70 percent of the world's HIV cases were in Africa—primarily in sub-Saharan Africa (the portion of Africa south of the Sahara Desert, including Kenya, Ethiopia, Uganda, and Tanzania). HIV, or the human immunodeficiency virus, is the retrovirus that causes AIDS. About one-third of all adults in Botswana and one-fourth of adults in Zimbabwe (both in Africa) have HIV or AIDS.

In the early 1980s, a person with AIDS could expect to die within a year or two of diagnosis. In the late 1990s, however, researchers developed powerful drugs that could slow the progress of AIDS and extend the lives of people with AIDS for several years. As the twentieth century came to a close, health advocates were working to make these expensive drugs affordable for public health agencies and patients in poor countries. Medical officials were also seeking a vaccine that would prevent new cases of HIV infection.

Mural displaying a public service announcement about HIV and AIDS in Thokosa, a township outside Johannesburg, South Africa. **(Reproduced by permission of Getty Images.)**

Lifetimes of cancer patients extended

By the end of the twentieth century, one in three people in industrialized countries could expect to develop cancer at some point in their lifetime. In the United States, cancer—along with heart disease and stroke—replaced infectious, epidemic diseases as the leading causes of death. In the 1990s, almost one in four American deaths were due to cancer.

While cancer has been around for centuries, it was only in the latter half of the twentieth century that scientists began to understand its causes and develop effective treatments. As a result, the survival rates of cancer patients increased dramatically from the 1940s to the 1990s. Between 1990 and 1997, the overall death rate from cancer in the United States dropped. Despite billions of dollars spent on cancer research, however, at the end of the century there was still no cure or vaccine for cancer.

Organ transplantation offers second chance at life

Organ transplantation, surgically implanting a healthy internal organ into a patient, began in the mid-twentieth century. This very difficult procedure provides a second chance at life for people facing death due to the failure of a major organ (primarily the kidneys, liver, heart, lungs, and pancreas). While at first these operations had a low success rate, by the early 1980s transplants were meeting with greater success and had entered the mainstream of medicine. That improvement was largely due to the development of cyclosporin and other drugs that prevent the patient's immune system from attacking the new organ. Today between 80 and 95 percent (depending on the type of organ transplanted) of organ recipients live longer than a year after their operation, and more than 75 percent of successful transplant recipients can return to the life they enjoyed before they became ill.

Toward the end of the century the demand was much greater than the supply of organs for transplant. In the year 2000, more than 67,000 people in the United States were on a waiting list to receive organs, while there were only about 5,000 donors per year. As a result, about fifteen people die each day while awaiting organ transplants.

The shortage of organs for transplantation has raised some important ethical questions, such as how to decide which people should receive the life-saving organs. Doctors also must decide when a potential donor is beyond help and how far they should go in attempting to save the lives of potential donors. And as the shortage of organs has created a possible black market, society must determine how to prevent the sale or purchase of organs. Organ transplantation is as much a social concern as a medical one, as health professionals struggle to talk people into promising to donate their organs.

High-tech tools look inside the body

In the second half of the twentieth century a number of high-tech imaging devices emerged that could see inside the body and help doctors diagnose diseases and injuries. These tools—including magnetic resonance imaging (MRI), ultrasound, computed tomography (CT) scanning, and X-ray machines—allow physicians to explore the body without using surgery. These advances in imaging technology were made possible by the growth of computer capabilities as well as developments in physics and mathematics. High-tech imaging equipment has made diagnoses more accurate, safer, and more affordable.

The X-ray machine was the first device used to look inside the body and photograph bones and internal organs. CT scanning, introduced in 1972, produces a three-dimensional, detailed image of the brain and other internal organs. Ultrasound, which by the 1980s was being commonly used to monitor fetal development in pregnant women, uses high-frequency sound waves to see inside the body. And MRI (formerly called nuclear magnetic resonance [NMR]) was first used in the late 1960s. MRI produces pictures of bones, tissues, and organs, as well as the structures of large molecules and compounds, by exposing atoms to a strong magnetic field and radio waves and observing the atoms' response.

Birth control methods made available

One of the most significant, and most controversial, health advances in the twentieth century was birth control. The century saw an explosion of methods by which women could control their fertility, beginning with the birth control pill in 1960 and continuing through RU-486 (the French abortion pill) in the 1980s.

Birth control, it turned out, is not just a medical matter; it is also a social and ethical one. Some religious groups opposed birth control, insisting that it would encourage immoral behavior and that humans should leave conception up to God. The most heated debate focused on abortion, the expulsion or removal of an embryo or fetus from the womb. Ever since the U.S. Supreme Court ruled that abortion was legal in the 1973 decision *Roe v. Wade,* anti-abortion groups have attempted to reverse the decision.

Despite the moral concerns of some conservative groups, birth control has made a significant difference in women's lives. Women can now choose to put off or forgo having children in order to finish school, establish a career, or accomplish other goals. Women have also given birth to fewer children, on average, since the introduction of safe and effective birth control.

ESSAYS

☐ THE DEVELOPMENT OF PUBLIC HEALTH SERVICES

Overview

Public health is the branch of medicine concerned with preventing disease, promoting health, and prolonging life. It deals with the physical, mental, social, and environmental health of entire communities. Examples of public health actions include water and sewage sanitation, vaccination campaigns against contagious diseases, food safety monitoring, and personal hygiene education. Public health agencies also advise the government on passing laws that ensure the safety of workers and the health of the general population.

Central to public health is the field of epidemiology, which is concerned with epidemic diseases (diseases with a rapid increase in the rate of infection). Epidemiologists collect and analyze data from state and local health departments and look for connections between diseases and factors such as diet, lifestyle patterns, and the environment. Public health workers then act upon that information to halt the spread of disease.

Public health agencies in the United States and throughout the world boasted many accomplishments during the twentieth century. Vaccination campaigns wiped out smallpox and greatly reduced the incidence of polio, diphtheria, and other diseases. Educational efforts decreased the number of cases of other diseases, from dysentery (an infectious disease whose symptoms include uncontrolled diarrhea and dehydration) to acquired immunodeficiency syndrome (AIDS; a fatal disease characterized by a weakened immune system, which leaves the patient unable to fight off other illnesses). (See essay The AIDS Pandemic in this chapter.)

Background

Most industrialized nations, and many developing nations, now have public health agencies that research and analyze health trends and carry out programs to protect and improve public health. Public health efforts occurred now and then throughout history. One of the earliest examples was the construction of sewers to prevent human contact with raw sewage, which can carry many diseases, in ancient Rome. (After the fall of the Roman Empire in C.E. 476, the sewer systems fell into disrepair and were largely nonexistent until the 1800s.)

Public health systems grew during the nineteenth century, along with advances in medical science. In the 1860s, for instance, English surgeon Joseph Lister (1827–1912) used the discovery that bacteria spread illness and infection to improve cleanliness procedures in hospitals. And in the twentieth century, public health efforts were aided by the development of vaccines and antibiotics to prevent and treat diseases (see essay The Discovery, Importance, and Limitations of Antibiotics in this chapter), as well as the discovery of the role that diet, vitamins, and exercise play in keeping a person healthy (see essay The Discovery of Vitamins and Their Relationship to Good Health in this chapter).

antibiotics: a class of drugs that fight infections caused by bacteria.

endemic disease: a disease that normally occurs in a population at a relatively constant rate.

epidemic disease: a disease with a rapid increase in the rate of infection.

epidemiology: the branch of medicine concerned with epidemic diseases.

public health: the branch of medicine concerned with efforts to prevent disease, promote health, and prolong life in communities.

sewage system: a system of treating sewage (wastewater) to acceptable standards of cleanliness before discharging it into lakes or rivers.

vaccination: (also called inoculation or immunization) the process of injecting weakened or dead bacteria or viruses into a person to protect them from a specific disease.

Formation of the World Health Organization

International cooperation on public health issues began in the mid-1800s with the International Sanitary Congress, a series of meetings held throughout Europe and the United States. The effort was largely caused by concerns over the rapid spread of fatal diseases. In the early 1900s two international bodies formed: the Pan-American Sanitary Bureau in Washington, D.C., and the International Office of Public Hygiene in Paris, France. When the League of Nations was created after World War I (1914–18), it established a health organization based in Geneva, Switzerland.

In 1948, the United Nations (UN), which replaced the League of Nations after World War II (1939–45), founded a new international public health agency: the World Health Organization (WHO). The new organization's stated mission was to achieve for all people "the highest possible level of health." In its constitution, WHO defines health as "a state of complete physical, mental, and social well-being and not merely the absence of disease or infirmity."

During the 1950s and 1960s, the WHO's vaccination and health education campaigns in the developing world led to a drop in the rates of both endemic (normally occurring in a population at a relatively constant rate) and epidemic diseases, including cholera, trachoma, yellow fever, tuberculosis, malaria, and venereal disease. WHO staff members also trained health workers in developing countries to gather and analyze health data and helped them establish national public health programs.

At the end of the twentieth century, the WHO was coordinating the activities of regional public health committees throughout the world. The organization also provided information, held conferences, and conducted health campaigns on topics such as disease outbreaks, health emergencies, cancer research, health advice and vaccination requirements for travelers, mental health, the latest developments in vaccines, the effect of poverty on health, the health needs of refugees, and water supplies.

Formation of the U.S. Public Health Service

In the United States, the Public Health Service (PHS) of the Department of Health and Human Services is the principal health agency. The PHS has its roots in 1798, when Congress passed a law creating the Marine Hospital Service (MHS) to care for sailors and merchant seamen. The Department of the Treasury controlled the new agency. The following year saw the construction of the first government-owned hospital. In the coming decades, the MHS also began to aid crews on boats and rafts on domestic waterways (such as the Mississippi River and the Great Lakes).

In 1870, Congress reorganized the MHS and appointed a surgeon, Dr. John M. Woodworth, as director. Woodworth employed a mobile team of health experts and supported the developing public health movement. He also helped draft the first federal quarantine law in 1878, which set out standard procedures for isolating individuals with contagious diseases to prevent them from infecting others.

The mission of the MHS continued to expand; in the 1890s it oversaw medical examinations and quarantine for newly arrived immigrants. In 1902 the name of the agency was changed to the United States Public Health and Marine Hospital Service, to reflect its broader concerns. The name was shortened to United States Public Health Service in 1912.

Today the PHS, which is headed by the U.S. Surgeon General, includes the Food and Drug Administration, the Centers for Disease Control, the Bureau of Medical Services, the National Institutes of Health, and the National Library of Medicine. The arms of the PHS work together to prevent diseases from abroad from entering the country; to provide medical services to military personnel, veterans, and Native Americans; to protect the purity of

Jonas Salk and the
Polio Vaccine

Jonas Salk innoculating a young child during polio vaccine field trials, 1954. (Courtesy of the Library of Congress.)

American microbiologist (a scientist who studies the structure, function, and uses of microscopic organisms) Jonas Salk (1914–1995) developed the first vaccine for polio (a crippling viral disease, often affecting children, that leads to permanent partial paralysis and deformities) in 1954. His discovery came at a time when the United States was suffering from a polio epidemic; some 47,000 people had been infected.

Salk studied the poliomyelitis virus (the virus that causes polio) at the Virus Research Laboratory at the University of Pittsburgh School of Medicine, with the backing of the National Foundation for Infantile Paralysis. There he grew the virus in cultures of monkey kidney tissue and then killed the virus. Tests on humans showed that the dead virus safely and effectively protected people against polio. The vaccine was quickly approved and led to a significant decrease in the number of polio cases worldwide.

Salk's vaccine was improved in 1957, when physician Albert Bruce Sabin (1906–1993) developed a form that could be taken through the mouth. Sabin's live-virus vaccine was easier to give than Salk's (it merely required placing drops of liquid on the tongue), only needed a single dose to work, and gave vaccinated patients a stronger immunity to the disease. Vaccination campaigns in the United States were so effective that in 1981 only six cases of polio were reported in the country, compared with more than 20,000 a year before the vaccine was developed.

foods, drugs, and cosmetics; and to regulate the production of vaccines and other medicines. The PHS and its member organizations also support medical research and health services, work with other countries on international health matters, and sponsor educational programs throughout the country.

Impact

Public health programs made a huge positive impact on the lives of people around the world in the twentieth century. Water treatment, particularly in industrialized nations, almost eliminated diseases such as typhoid and cholera that are carried by water. In some less-developed nations, however, where much of the population still drinks untreated water, those diseases remain a threat. During a five-year period in the early 1990s, outbreaks of waterborne diseases killed more than 3 million infants and children around the world.

Some of the twentieth century's greatest public health achievements were in the fight against infectious diseases. The development of antibiotics, drugs that fight infections caused by bacteria, provided a cure for nearly every bacterial illness. Antibiotics lost some of their effectiveness in the 1970s, however, when strains of resistant bacteria began to emerge (see essay The Discovery, Importance, and Limitations of Antibiotics in this chapter).

Another twentieth-century accomplishment was the development of vaccines for a number of nonbacterial infectious diseases, such as smallpox, polio, diphtheria, rabies, measles, cholera, and chicken pox. Vaccination campaigns have decreased or destroyed many diseases that once affected large numbers of people. As a result of global vaccination efforts, by the end of the century 80 percent of the world's children had been vaccinated against major childhood diseases, and child mortality dropped sharply.

Challenges for the twenty-first century

Public health workers in the twenty-first century face some major challenges, in particular halting the spread of AIDS, fighting the effects of poverty and war on human health, and increasing the supply of safe water. In addition, public health workers must deal with tuberculosis and some types of hepatitis that re-emerged in the 1990s. Public health professionals are also continuing efforts to reduce deaths caused by heart disease and stroke, to discourage smoking, and to protect the public from pollutants in the air and water.

☐ THE DISCOVERY OF VITAMINS AND THEIR RELATIONSHIP TO GOOD HEALTH

Overview

Vitamins are organic (derived from living matter) compounds that are essential in the diets of humans and other animals for growth, maintaining

beriberi: a disease caused by a deficiency of thiamine and characterized by nerve and gastrointestinal disorders.

germ theory of disease: the belief that disease is caused by germs (microorganisms).

pellagra: a disease caused by a deficiency of niacin and characterized by severe skin problems and diarrhea.

rickets: a bone-weakening disease caused by a deficiency of vitamin D.

scurvy: a disease caused by a deficiency of vitamin C, in which connective tissue in bone and muscle is weakened, resulting in bleeding gums, bruising, and severe weakness.

vitamins: organic substances found mainly in foods that are essential in small quantities for growth and health.

life functions, and preventing disease. Vitamins help control the body's metabolism (the rate at which the body changes into usable energy) and help form hormones, blood, bones, skin, glands, and nerves. Of the vitamins vital to human health, only vitamin D is produced by the body; all others must be obtained through food.

Throughout history, people around the world have suffered from diseases caused by not getting enough vitamins. While scientists had long suspected a link between diet and health, it was not until the twentieth century that they discovered vitamins and determined how vitamins helped people fight disease and maintain health.

Background

As early as ancient Greece, people believed that specific foods could cure certain health problems. The Greek physician Hippocrates (c. 460–377 B.C.E.), for example, recommended that people with poor vision should eat beef liver. Scientists have since discovered that liver contains vitamin A, which maintains the health of the retina and aids vision.

In the 1700s English naval surgeon James Lind (1716–1794) discovered the link between scurvy—a disease whose symptoms include bleeding gums, bruising, and severe weakness—and certain foods. British sailors, who were at sea for long periods without access to fresh fruits and vegetables, developed the disease in high numbers. In 1754, Lind recommended that the British navy provide its sailors with fresh fruits and vegetables while at sea. Lemons and limes were the fruits of choice since they lasted a long time; the latter led to a new nickname for British sailors: "limeys." Doctors later learned that scurvy is caused by a lack of vitamin C in the diet and that some fresh fruits and vegetables, particularly citrus fruits, contain vitamin C.

In the second half of the nineteenth century the germ theory of disease—the belief that diseases are caused by microorganisms, or germs, which was developed by French chemist Louis Pasteur (1822–1895) and German physician Robert Koch (1843–1910)—revolutionized the medical field. As a result, the diet-disease connection was pushed to the background. Between 1879 and 1900, scientists were discovering microorganisms responsible for many of the world's most serious diseases at a rate of more than one per year. They believed at the time that diseases such as pellagra and beriberi were caused by germs, when in fact they are caused by vitamin deficiencies.

Research conducted on diet-disease link

One of the earliest scientific studies on the link between diet and disease was conducted by Christiaan Eijkman (1858–1930; see box on page 206) in 1886. Eijkman found that a substance in the hulls of brown rice, which was later identified as thiamine, could prevent and cure beriberi (a disease characterized by nerve and gastrointestinal disorders).

English biochemist Frederick Gowland Hopkins, who demonstrated the existence of essential amino acids and of accessory food factors later called vitamins. (Reproduced by permission of AP/Wide World Photos.)

Two decades later, British biochemist Frederick Gowland Hopkins (1861–1947) discovered that milk contains substances necessary for animals' health. At Cambridge University in 1906, Hopkins experimented on young rats. He fed the rats starch, sugar, salt, casein (a protein found in milk that forms the basis of cheese), and lard—everything believed necessary for life at the time. One group of rats also received milk, and developed normally. The rats that did not have milk failed to thrive. Hopkins

Christiaan Eijkman and the Discovery of Vitamins

Christiaan Eijkman.
(Reproduced by permission of the Corbis Corporation.)

Dutch bacteriologist (a scientist who studies bacteria) Christiaan Eijkman (1858–1930) paved the way for the discovery of vitamins by studying the cause of beriberi in the Dutch East Indies (today called Indonesia). Beriberi is characterized by nerve and gastrointestinal disorders, severe muscular weakness, pain in and paralysis of the arms and legs, emaciation (weight loss) or swelling of the body, and heart failure. At the time of Eijkman's 1886 study, beriberi was common in rice-growing regions throughout Asia.

Eijkman, who was the director of the medical school and research laboratory in Batavia (now the capital city of Jakarta), conducted his study at the

came to the conclusion that there were certain "accessory substances" (later identified as several vitamins) in milk that were necessary for growth and health.

In 1912 Polish-American biochemist Casimir Funk (1884–1967) isolated the substance in rice hulls that protects against beriberi. He called it "vitamine," from the Latin word *vita*, meaning "life," and "amine," a compound derived from ammonia. Funk's research began the quest to identify particular vitamins. In following years, the term was shortened to "vitamin."

The search for a cure for pellagra

In the early 1900s, pellagra—a disease characterized by skin eruptions, diarrhea, dementia, and sometimes death—was widespread throughout facility's hospital. The hospital fed its patients processed white rice from which the hulls had been removed. Eijkman experimented with chickens, which normally ate brown rice (with the hull still attached), and began feeding them white rice instead. The chickens eventually developed a form of beriberi, from which they recovered when they began eating brown rice again. Eijkman concluded that beriberi was caused by the lack of some substance in the hulls of brown rice.

Eijkman conducted the second part of his study at a prison on the Indonesian island of Java. There, some prisoners were fed white rice and others brown rice. He found that about two-thirds of the prisoners on the white-rice diet developed beriberi, compared with only a few of the prisoners on the brown-rice diet. He then produced an extract from the rice hulls that he believed could cure beriberi.

In 1926, scientists identified the healing substance as thiamine, a water-soluble B vitamin that is necessary for the nervous system to function normally. Eijkman won the Nobel Prize in physiology or medicine in 1929 for his role in the discovery of vitamins.

the southern United States. South Carolina, with 30,000 cases, was hardest hit; 40 percent of the people who contracted the disease died. Hungarian-American physician Joseph Goldberger (1874–1929), a surgeon with the U.S. Marine Hospital Service (later renamed the U.S. Public Health Service; see essay The Development of Public Health Services in this chapter) went to the South in search of a cure in 1914.

Goldberger at first suspected that pellagra was an infectious disease, but he observed that people who ate a well-balanced diet did not come down with pellagra. He also noted that neither he nor his assistants, all of whom spent a great deal of time with pellagra patients, got the disease. These facts led Goldberger to believe that pellagra was not spread by a germ but was rather the result of a poor diet.

Goldberger then conducted experiments in which he gave children in orphanages fresh meats, vegetables and milk, instead of their usual corn-based diet, with remarkable results. Children with pellagra recovered, and newly arriving residents did not contract the disease. In a dramatic gesture, to prove pellagra was not a contagious disease, Goldberger and an assistant injected themselves with blood from pellagra patients; neither of them developed the disease. Goldberger blamed the high rate of pellagra on the economic system in the South, in which wealthy landowners paid tenant farmers so little they could not afford to buy healthy foods.

In 1937 Albert Szent-Györgyi was awarded the Nobel Prize in physiology or medicine for his work in isolating vitamin C and his advances in the study of intercellular respiration. (Courtesy of the Library of Congress.)

Vitamins identified and described

Researchers made tremendous gains in the 1920s and 1930s in their understanding of the role vitamins play in health. In 1922, scientists identified vitamin D and showed that it prevents rickets, a bone-weakening disease that particularly affects children (in 1900 an estimated 80 percent of children in Boston had rickets). The year 1926 saw the identification of niacin, which prevents and cures pellagra, and thiamine, which prevents beriberi. In 1933, Hungarian-American biochemist Albert Szent-Györgyi (1893–1986) discovered vitamin C (which keeps the skin, bones, teeth, and muscles healthy), for which he won the Nobel Prize in physiology or medicine in 1937. Szent-Györgyi also lectured widely on the importance of vitamins for maintaining health. And in 1943, American biochemist Edward A. Doisy (1893–1986) and Danish biochemist Henrik Dam (1895–1976) shared the Nobel Prize in physiology or medicine for their discovery of vitamin K (which prevents excessive bleeding by helping to clot blood).

Impact

Scientific research into vitamins made clear the importance of good nutrition for maintaining health. Along with these major discoveries about vitamins came increased attention to the problems of poverty and malnutrition. Famine was widespread throughout the developing world, and hunger was common even in the United States during the Great Depression (a period of severe economic downturn; 1929–1939). After World War II (1939–45), there were pockets of famine in countries that had been involved in the war.

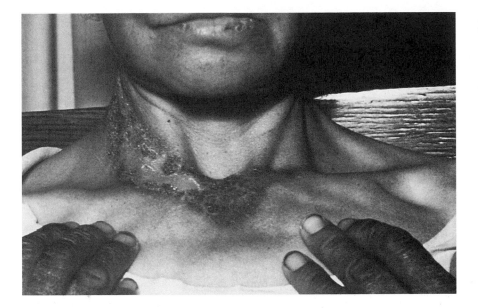

Symptoms of pellagra, a disease caused by niacin deficiency.
(Reproduced by permission of the Corbis Corporation.)

To combat world hunger and malnutrition, the United Nations—the world governance body formed after World War II—established the Food and Agriculture Organization (FAO) to help increase food production, improve nutrition, and distribute emergency food supplies. The FAO was founded on the belief that an adequate food supply was essential to preventing war as well as to fighting disease.

Improvement of health

The National Academy of Sciences, an organization of scientists and engineers that advises the government on science and technology, created guidelines for the recommended daily allowances (RDAs) of certain vitamins and minerals in 1941. By 1950, vitamin pills specially designed for children, adults, and pregnant women became commercially available. Manufacturers of cereals, grains, flour, bread, and milk also began adding certain vitamins to their products. In the latter half of the 1900s, pellagra, beriberi, scurvy, and other diseases caused by vitamin deficiencies almost disappeared in the United States and other industrialized nations. In poor countries, however, large numbers of people continued to suffer from those health problems.

☐ THE DISCOVERY, IMPORTANCE, AND LIMITATIONS OF ANTIBIOTICS

Overview

Antibiotics are a class of drugs that fight infections caused by bacteria. The word *antibiotic* means "against life," referring to antibiotics' ability to

antibiotics: a class of drugs, derived from living organisms such as fungi, molds, and certain soil bacteria, that fight infections and infectious diseases caused by bacteria.

penicillin: a chemical produced in common molds that has strong antibacterial properties; it can treat a broad range of bacterial infections in humans.

resistant bacteria: a strain of bacteria that over time has become immune to an antibiotic's effect.

sulfa drugs: also called sulfanilamides; the first chemicals used to treat bacterial infections, they are distilled from dyes that bind tightly to wool.

synthetic antibiotics: antibiotics that are made in a laboratory, in which the basic molecule of the naturally occurring substance is chemically altered.

destroy living bacteria. Antibiotics first became available during World War II (1939–45) and were at first seen as miracle drugs because they could cure what had previously been life-threatening conditions. For instance, before penicillin (one of the earliest antibiotics), between 60 and 80 percent of pneumonia patients died; since doctors began using penicillin, the death rate for pneumonia patients dropped to between 1 and 5 percent.

Antibiotics are created from living organisms such as fungi, molds, and certain soil bacteria. The drugs work either by destroying the cell membranes (the thin outer layer) of harmful bacteria and preventing the bacteria from reproducing, or by keeping the bacteria from producing necessary proteins. In addition to antibiotics from natural sources, today many types of antibiotics are synthesized (manufactured) in laboratories.

Antibiotics are heavily used around the world to fight a variety of infections. In recent years, however, the overuse and misuse of antibiotics have led to new strains of bacteria that are resistant to antibiotics. As a result, there are now certain bacterial illnesses for which there is no cure.

Background

While humans have suffered from diseases throughout history, it was not until the seventeenth century that scientists learned that microscopic organisms existed and could cause illness. Before that time, people believed that disease was caused by evil spirits or by the will of the gods. Some believed that illness was divine punishment for bad behavior or a sign of troubled times to come.

In the mid-1800s, French chemist Louis Pasteur (1822–1895), using one of the first complex microscopes, discovered the existence of living bacteria and explained that bacteria and other microorganisms cause disease by entering the human body and multiplying. Bacteria, we now know, are single-celled organisms that exist everywhere in nature. While most types of bacteria are harmless to humans, there are several that cause illness. Bacteria enter the human body through the nose, the mouth, or a wound and cause diseases such as pneumonia, tuberculosis, typhoid fever, cholera, and strep throat.

Sulfa drugs

The first chemicals used to treat bacterial infections were sulfanilamides (pronounced sul-fuh-NILL-uh-midze), also called sulfa drugs. In 1908 scientists discovered that certain substances in the dyes that were used to make cloth can also bind to bacteria. Researchers then set out to develop a usable form of the chemicals. It was not until 1932 that German bacteriologist (a scientist who studies bacteria) Gerhard Domagk (1895–1964) isolated the first sulfa drug that could treat bacterial ailments in humans, which he called Prontosil.

Sulfas were seen as wonder drugs, since there had never before been a medicine that could treat bacterial infections and diseases. The drugs saved many lives throughout the 1930s, before better antibiotics became available. Soon, however, sulfa drugs' drawbacks became apparent; for instance, they were highly toxic (poisonous), and their use over a long period of time could damage a patient's kidneys. Another problem was that sulfa drugs were used so widely that many strains of bacteria became resistant to their effects (see "Bacteria develop resistance to antibiotics" on page 214). Today, sulfa drugs are most commonly used to treat urinary tract infections.

Gerhard Domagk, a biochemist who discovered sulfonamide therapy for bacterial infections. (Courtesy of the Library of Congress.)

Discovery and purification of penicillin

The next antibiotic to be used against bacterial infection in humans was penicillin. Scottish bacteriologist Sir Alexander Fleming (1881–1955; see box on page 214) first recognized the potential anti-bacterial properties of penicillin in 1928. Fleming was conducting experiments that involved growing bacteria in dishes. One of the dishes, which contained a culture of staphylococcus bacteria, was accidentally left uncovered. The dish developed a patch of green mold around which no bacteria grew. The mold was the *Penicillium notatum* fungus, a substance closely related to the mold that grows on bread.

Fleming then experimented on mice, injecting them with a liquid mixture that contained penicillin. He found that the injection killed certain types of bacteria inside the mice without harming the animals. While Fleming realized that penicillin could treat human infections, he could not purify the substance in large enough quantities for that use.

It was not until 1940 that Australian-English pathologist (a scientist who studies diseases) Howard Florey (1898–1968) and German biochemist (a scientist who studies the chemistry of living things) Boris Ernst Chain (1906–1979) purified, tested, and developed penicillin for human use. In 1942, penicillin was first produced in large quantities in British factories, and in 1944 the first large-scale penicillin-production plant in the United States opened its doors. The drug saved the lives of countless soldiers in World War II who might otherwise have died from infections. Fleming, Florey, and Chain jointly received the Nobel Prize in physiology or medicine in 1945 for their work in developing penicillin.

British pathologist Howard Florey, who, with Ernst Chain, isolated and purified penicillin for general clinical use in 1939. (Reproduced by permission of the Corbis Corporation.)

Penicillin is used to treat many bacterial diseases, including pneumonia, strep throat, scarlet fever, gonorrhea and syphilis (venereal diseases), meningitis (a disease that affects the brain and spinal cord), and impetigo (a contagious skin disease). The discovery of penicillin also aided the development of other useful antibiotics.

Streptomycin

Penicillin cured many diseases; however, there were some types of bacteria it could not affect. Russian-American microbiologist Selman Abraham Waksman (1888–1973), a professor at Rutgers University in New Jersey, was one of the scientists who continued to search for antibiotics that could treat other serious illnesses. In the early 1940s, Waksman isolated an antibacterial substance from the *Streptomyces griseus* fungus, which he called streptomycin. For his discovery of this drug, which cures the infectious lung disease tuberculosis, Waksman won the Nobel Prize in physiology or medicine in 1952.

Through the use of streptomycin, tuberculosis, which once was a serious public health threat, has been almost wiped out in the industrialized world. (The number of cases of tuberculosis in the developing world, however, was on the rise at the end of the twentieth century.) Streptomycin was also an effective treatment for pneumonia, spinal meningitis, and typhoid fever. Due to its overuse, however, many strains of bacteria have become resistant to streptomycin, and it has become less effective.

Synthetic antibiotics

After World War II, drug companies in the United States sought to mass-produce antibiotics in laboratories. They began searching the world for antibacterial molds and soil bacteria that could be synthesized, or created using nonliving materials. The first synthetic antibiotics produced, in the mid-1940s, were the tetracyclines, a class of drugs including aureomycin, erythromycin, terramycin, and other substances that can combat a wide range of bacterial illnesses. Tetracyclines often have unpleasant side effects such as dizziness, drowsiness, and nausea, so they are used only in certain cases.

Another important group of synthetic antibiotics are the cephalosporins: substances that have the same effects as penicillin. Cephalosporins are given to patients who are allergic to penicillin and to those who are infected with strains of bacteria that are resistant to penicillin.

Bacitracin, an ointment that fights skin infections, was synthetically produced in 1945. Two years later, chloramphenicol, an antibiotic that destroys many types of bacteria, was produced and widely prescribed. In the years since, researchers have developed many other synthetic antibiotics.

American biochemist Selman Waksman discovered the antibiotic streptomycin in 1943. **(Reproduced by permission of Archive Photos, Inc.)**

Impact

The development of antibiotics changed the way health and disease were regarded around the world. Bacterial diseases, previously seen as a death sentence, could suddenly be cured with a shot or a pill. The development

Sir Alexander Fleming.
(Reproduced by permission of
the Corbis Corporation.)

Scottish bacteriologist (a scientist who studies bacteria) Sir Alexander Fleming (1881–1955) received the Nobel Prize in physiology or medicine in 1945 along with Howard Florey and Boris Ernst Chain for his role in the discovery of penicillin. While that accomplishment represented the peak of Fleming's career, he also made other less famous discoveries, such as lysozyme, an antibacterial agent found in tears and saliva.

Fleming was educated at St. Mary's Hospital Medical School at the University of London, where he earned his medical degree in 1906. He stayed as a lecturer at St. Mary's until World War I (1914–18), when he served in the Royal Army Medical Corps; he returned to St. Mary's faculty after the war.

of antibiotics also encouraged researchers to search for treatments for other types of serious diseases.

By the end of the twentieth century, however, many types of antibiotics had become ineffective due to the development of resistant strains of bacteria (see below). Another drawback of antibiotics was their side effects, which ranged from skin rashes to kidney damage. In short, antibiotics, while still of immense importance in treating many diseases, are no longer seen as magical cure-alls.

Bacteria develop resistance to antibiotics
The main cause for the evolution of resistant strains of bacteria (bacteria that over time become immune to antibiotics' effects) is the overuse of

In 1928, the same year Fleming became a lecturer at the Royal College of Surgeons, he was experimenting with the staphylococcus bacteria when a mold called *Penicillium notatum* accidentally grew on one of his culture plates. Fleming analyzed the mold and found that it killed many types of bacteria in animals without harming them. He published the results of his experiments in 1929, in which he suggested that penicillin could be useful in treating disease. Fleming could not isolate enough of penicillin's antibacterial substance to conduct large-scale tests, however, and the medical community largely ignored penicillin for the next decade.

Interest in penicillin increased during World War II (1939–45), when soldiers with infected wounds and bacterial illnesses needed an antibacterial cure. European researchers Howard Florey (1898–1968) and Boris Ernst Chain (1906–1979) obtained a sample of Fleming's *Penicillium notatum* and came up with a way to produce the antibacterial substance in large quantities. Penicillin successfully treated large numbers of soldiers.

Fleming became a member of England's prestigious Royal Society in 1943 and was knighted in 1944. He became emeritus professor (a position of honor for retired faculty) of bacteriology (the study of bacteria) at the University of London in 1948, where he remained until his death in 1955.

antibiotics—in particular, giving antibiotics to patients who have no bacterial infections. Studies conducted in the late 1990s found that doctors commonly prescribed antibiotics for colds, flus, and other illnesses caused by viruses, which antibiotics do not affect. One 1997 study at the University of Colorado found that 21 percent of all antibiotics prescribed in the United States were not necessary.

Bacteria also gain resistance through the misuse of antibiotics. Misuse typically means that the patient does not take the full dose of the antibiotic over the time period prescribed. This creates bacteria that have been exposed to, but not killed by, the antibiotics. Those bacteria are more likely to produce offspring that are resistant to antibiotics.

Another factor is the routine feeding of antibiotics to livestock. Almost half of the antibiotics sold in the United States are mixed into the food or water given to livestock to keep the animals from getting sick and make them grow faster. This speeds the evolution of resistant bacteria and puts the effectiveness of antibiotics in humans at risk.

☐ ISSUES AND DEVELOPMENTS IN BIRTH CONTROL

Overview

The twentieth century saw huge advances in the range and quality of birth control methods. Scientific gains, however, did not always mean increased availability and choices for women. Even after some medical technologies for preventing pregnancy were developed, political and ethical considerations restricted their use.

The introduction of the birth control pill in 1960 was the start of a scientific and social revolution and heralded the development of other methods of preventing pregnancy. In 1961 the intrauterine device (IUD) became available, and around 1990 implants that slowly released pregnancy-preventing hormones hit the market. The most controversial birth-control method of all, a pill called RU-486 (the French abortion pill), was developed in 1980 but twenty years later was available in the United States only for restricted use.

Much of the debate over birth control in the United States has focused on abortion, the expulsion or removal of an embryo or fetus from the womb. The 1973 U.S. Supreme Court decision *Roe v. Wade* ruled that abortion was legal. Since that decision, the battle has raged between those who believe abortion is essentially murder and those who view the right to abortion as the right of women to control their bodies and their lives.

Background

Before the nineteenth century, very little information existed about the human reproductive system or how to prevent pregnancies. While some women used folk remedies to prevent or end pregnancy, many women merely accepted the fact that they would have large families. The delivery

British biochemist Ernest Chain, who, along with Howard Florey and Sir Alexander Fleming, received the Nobel Prize in physiology or medicine for their discovery of penicillin. (Reproduced by permission of the Corbis Corporation.)

of babies and care for pregnant women was mainly handled by female health workers called midwives.

Family planning and birth control began to change in the 1800s, as scientists gained a greater understanding of the human body and fertility. That period also saw the distribution of family-planning educational materials and research into birth control. Another change in the 1800s was that male medical doctors trained in obstetrics (the branch of medical science concerned with childbirth and caring for and treating women in connection with childbirth) began to replace midwives.

Birth control information restricted

The new interest in fertility meant it was necessary to talk frankly about sex, which was considered unacceptable by Victorian society. People opposed to family planning organized campaigns against it. Leading the movement in the United States was the Society for the Suppression of Vice, an organization headed by political reformer and anti-pornography crusader Anthony Comstock (1844–1915). Comstock argued that contraception, like pornography, was immoral.

Comstock's group persuaded Congress to pass the Comstock Law in 1873, which made it illegal for doctors to discuss birth control with their patients. Specifically, the legislation outlawed the making, transportation, or distribution of "obscene, lewd, and lascivious matter."

Stopes and Sanger turn the tide

Between 1873 and 1936, the Comstock Law slowed but failed to stop efforts to educate the public about birth control. American nurse Margaret Sanger (1879–1966; see box on page 218), who invented the term "birth control," illegally taught working-class women in New York City how to prevent unwanted pregnancies. Sanger's cause attracted many followers, and in 1921 they formed the American Birth Control League (which later became Planned Parenthood). In Great Britain, meanwhile, social reformer Marie Carmichael Stopes (1880–1958) led the struggle for access to information about reproduction. Stopes opened the country's first birth control clinic in 1921.

English paleobotanist, birth control advocate, and author Marie Charlotte Carmichael Stopes. (Courtesy of the Library of Congress.)

The birth control pill

After birth control information and services became legal in the United States, efforts increased to develop safe and effective methods for prevent-

Margaret Sanger:
Birth Control Pioneer

Margaret Sanger.
(Reproduced by permission of
the Planned Parenthood
Federation of America, Inc.)

American nurse Margaret Sanger (1879–1966) is considered the founder of the birth-control movement in the United States. In the early 1900s, while she was a health-care worker in the ghettos of New York City, she saw firsthand the consequences of the nation's birth control laws: large numbers of women dying from self-induced or illegal abortions, high rates of death among infants and mothers, and poor mothers burdened with more children than they could feed. Sanger believed that the answers to those problems lay in the ability of women to control their own reproduction.

In 1914 Sanger was charged with obscenity under the Comstock Law for distributing pamphlets supporting the legalization of birth control. In 1916, after the charge was dismissed, Sanger opened a birth control clinic in New York City. The police closed down the clinic, calling it a public nuisance, and kept Sanger in jail for thirty days in 1917.

Undiscouraged, Sanger continued her crusade. She founded the American Birth Control League in 1921, which worked for the legalization of birth control. In 1942, the Planned Parenthood Federation of America formed from a merger of the American Birth Control League and other organizations.

ing unwanted pregnancies. Perhaps the most important tool, which the Food and Drug Administration (FDA) approved for use in the United States in 1960, was the birth control pill. The pill was the first safe, easy-to-use, and reliable contraceptive.

In the early 1940s American chemist Russell Marker (1902–) discovered the steroid called progesterone in a yucca-like yam called the *cabeza de nigra,* which grew only in Mexico. (Progesterone sparks the production of mucus, which resists sperm, and alters the lining of the uterus in a way that prevents a fertilized egg from implanting—thus preventing pregnancy.) He founded a company called Syntex to synthesize progesterone from the plant. Marker eventually became discouraged by the difficulties of working in Mexico and gave up his quest.

Soon after, however, a pair of researchers who were also interested in birth control, Dr. Gregory Pincus (1903–1967), director of the Worcester Foundation for Experimental Biology, and American gynecologist (a physician specializing in women's reproductive health) **John Rock** (1890–1984; see biography in this chapter), persuaded Marker to let them synthesize (make in a laboratory) the progesterone molecule. Once Pincus and Rock had developed the pill, they tested it in Puerto Rico and Haiti. (They felt it would be too difficult to conduct trials in the United States, where the pill would cause controversy.)

The FDA's approval of the pill added fuel to the debate over contraception. While women's rights advocates praised it, saying it would allow women to choose the size of their families, the pill's opponents claimed that effective contraception would encourage immorality by removing the risk of accidentally becoming pregnant. Several states passed laws banning the pill from being distributed. In 1965, however, the Supreme Court struck down those laws and ruled that contraception was a matter of personal privacy.

Intrauterine devices

Another birth control tool that became widespread in the late 1950s is the intrauterine device (IUD). IUDs are small copper or plastic devices that are inserted into the uterus using minor surgery. They work in two ways: by affecting how sperm move to prevent the egg from being fertilized; and, if the egg is fertilized, by preventing the egg from being implanted in the uterus. Depending on the type of IUD, it can be left in place from one to ten years.

The advantage of the IUD is that it is 95 percent to 98 percent effective at preventing pregnancy; however, it can cause severe pelvic infections in some users. That type of infection reduces the woman's ability to become pregnant later on. One type of IUD, the Dalkon Shield, was responsible for a particularly high rate of pelvic infections among its users in the early 1970s. The company that produced the Dalkon Shield, A.H. Robins, was hit with so many lawsuits that it went bankrupt. By 1998 there were only two types of IUDs available in the United States: a copper device that mechanically prevents the fertilization of eggs and lasts ten years, and a loop that slowly releases progesterone and must replaced every year.

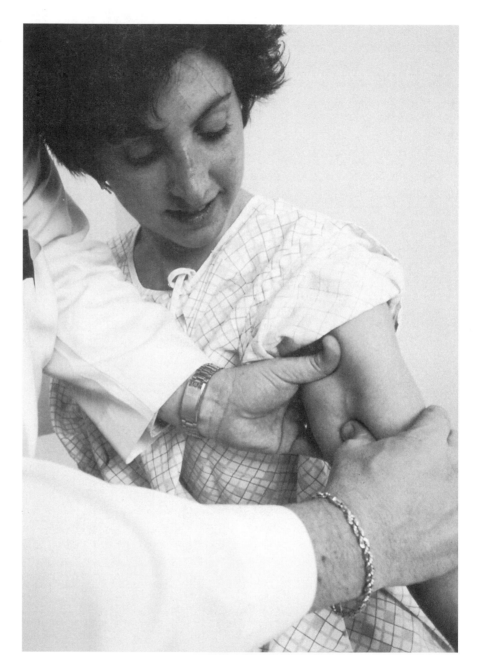

Doctor checking on a two-week-old Norplant birth control implant. (Reproduced by permission of Custom Medical Stock Photo, Inc.)

Roe v. Wade *makes abortion legal*

Abortion was legalized throughout the United States in 1973 by the Supreme Court decision *Roe v. Wade*. Prior to that time, abortion law had been left to individual states. The *Roe v. Wade* case was filed by a pregnant woman in Texas, using the alias "Roe," who wanted an abortion. At the time, the state of Texas outlawed abortion except in cases where the pregnancy would endanger the mother's life.

The Supreme Court ruled that the state of Texas could not force a woman to carry her fetus to term. By overturning Texas' restrictive abortion law, the Supreme Court also overturned antiabortion laws in other states. The court stated that women could end their pregnancies during the first trimester (three months), but left the question of abortion in the second and third trimesters up to individual states.

Norplant
In the 1990s, another birth control device, called Norplant, was introduced. Norplant consists of six match-sized rods that contain the hormones onorgestrol and progestin, which stop the ovaries from releasing eggs. These rods are inserted under the skin of the upper arm, where they slowly release the hormones for up to five years. Although Norplant is extremely effective—it prevents pregnancy in 99.9 percent of cases—it has unpleasant side effects, such as increased menstrual bleeding and headaches. In the late 1990s concerns arose over a possible link between Norplant and cancer. This led to numerous lawsuits against Norplant's manufacturer, Wyeth-Ayerst Laboratories, and caused Norplant's popularity to drop sharply.

Impact
The development of the birth control pill and other forms of pregnancy prevention has had a tremendous impact on society. Family planning choices have made a great difference in women's lives. The power to put off or decide against having children gives women the freedom to finish school, establish a career, or accomplish other goals. Since birth control and abortion have become available, women on average have chosen to have fewer children than in the past.

The debate surrounding birth control, and especially abortion, continued to rage at the start of the twenty-first century. The struggle pits family planning advocates, feminists, and scientists against religious and conservative groups. Central to the debate is the definition of life: in general, people opposed to birth control and abortion define life as beginning with conception (the fertilization of an egg by a sperm) and argue that humans should not interfere with that process. People who support family planning generally believe that life begins at the point when a fetus can survive outside the womb and argue that women's control of their fertility is central to control of their lives.

The abortion debate
Ever since *Roe v. Wade,* conservative forces have been trying to outlaw abortion. In 1974, Senators Jesse Helms and James Buckley proposed an

unsuccessful constitutional amendment to ban abortion. The antiabortion National Right to Life movement, together with the Catholic Church and other groups, have continued to push to restrict and ultimately end legal abortions.

In the mid 1980s, antiabortion demonstrators began holding frequent protests in front of clinics where abortions were performed. The vigils have been marked by heated confrontations between pro- and antiabortion forces, and there have been many acts of vandalism at clinics. There has been violence as well: three doctors, one volunteer, two receptionists, and one security guard were killed at abortion clinics in the United States in the 1990s.

Protesters against abortion at "March for Life" rally, 1975. (Reproduced by permission of AP/Wide World Photos.)

The powerful antiabortion lobby has persuaded several states to restrict abortions, such as preventing government-sponsored health programs from paying for abortions for poor women, establishing a waiting period during which a woman must view pictures of fetuses before she can have an abortion, requiring that minors have permission from a parent or

guardian to obtain an abortion, and limiting the length of time (such as up to the second trimester, or twenty-four weeks) during which a pregnant woman may have an abortion.

Introduction of RU-486 intensifies battle

RU-486, the French abortion pill, opened a new chapter in the family planning debate. Invented in 1988, RU-486 ends a pregnancy up to its seventh week without surgery. It does this by blocking the hormone progesterone from the uterus; as a result, the uterine lining and the attached embryo slough (drop) off.

Antiabortion forces in the United States successfully blocked the marketing of the drug in this country until the end of the twentieth century, even as women in France, Britain, Sweden, and China were using it safely. The U.S. Food and Drug Administration (FDA) finally approved RU-486 for use in the United States in 2000. It was made available only to family planning and other medical clinics after a nonprofit group obtained the patent to the drug and hired an unidentified manufacturer to produce it. At the beginning of the twenty-first century, RU-486 was available at clinics in many cities.

☐ THE DEVELOPMENT OF ORGAN TRANSPLANTATION

Overview

An organ transplant is the surgical implantation of a healthy internal organ into a patient; the organ comes from a donor who is alive or recently deceased. Transplants are an option when a major organ is failing and does not respond to all other therapies, but the health of the patient is otherwise good. For patients who fall into this category, an organ transplant can give them a second chance at life. The organs most commonly transplanted include the kidney, liver, heart, lungs, and the pancreas.

Organ transplants began in the mid-twentieth century. While at first the success rates were low, by the early 1980s transplants had entered the mainstream of medicine, and their success rates had greatly improved. Organ transplantation has expanded the boundaries of medical science. The research and performance of human organ transplants has resulted in more Nobel Prize awards than any other medical field in history.

Organ transplantation also has sparked ethical debates in the medical community and in the public at large. Questions have been raised such as: How do we decide who receives donated organs? Should organs be harvested from brain-dead patients? How can we prevent the sale or purchase of organs on the black market? And how can we persuade more people to pledge donation of their organs after death?

immunosuppressant: a substance that weakens the immune system.

xenotransplantation: the process of transplanting animal organs (primarily from pigs) into humans.

Background

The first attempted human organ transplants were with kidneys, organs that have a relatively simple blood-supply system. Beginning in 1933 and through the early 1950s, there were several unsuccessful kidney transplants around the world. In most cases the patient died within days of the operation; in fact, the longest any patient survived was six months.

The first truly successful kidney transplantation took place in 1954 in Boston, Massachusetts, between a patient and a donor who were identical twins. (It is possible for live people to donate a kidney, since humans have two and can survive with just one.) The recipient lived for eight years before dying in 1962 of a heart attack. A team of doctors led by American surgeon Joseph Edward Murray (1919–) performed the operation. Murray had studied how the body accepts or rejects donor tissue and had learned that the greatest successes were between identical twins. Murray won the Nobel Prize in physiology or medicine in 1990 for his work in organ transplantation.

Between 1954 and 1966, twenty-three successful kidney transplants between identical twins took place at the same Boston hospital. However, kidney transplants between people who were not identical twins continued to fail. Doctors realized that in order for organ transplants to succeed on a large scale, they had to solve the problem of organ rejection by the recipient.

Overcoming organ rejection

Doctors involved in early transplantation efforts had suspected that the body's immune system somehow was responsible for the rejection of transplanted organs. The immune system saw the new organ as a foreign body that it should destroy. In the early 1960s, medical researchers discovered the existence of different types of human tissue (similar to the different blood types) and found that when donor and recipient had the same tissue type, the odds of the organ being rejected dropped.

Another breakthrough was the development of azathioprine, a drug that could weaken the immune system and stop it from attacking the new organ. Beginning in 1962, kidney transplant patients routinely received this drug, which significantly increased their survival rate.

In 1962 doctors performed the first successful kidney transplant from a deceased donor; the kidney functioned normally for 21 months. The ability to transplant organs from recently deceased donors is significant because they are the greatest source of organ donations.

In 1983 the U.S. Food and Drug Administration approved an immunosuppressant (a substance that weakens the immune system) called cyclosporin, which was far more effective than azathioprine. Since cyclosporin was introduced, people who have received kidney transplants have had a 94 percent chance of surviving for one year after the operation. By the late twentieth century, kidneys were the most commonly transplanted organ, and kidney transplants had become the standard treatment for end-stage renal (kidney) disease.

Liver transplants

The liver, due to its complex blood supply system, is much more difficult to transplant than the kidney. American surgeon **Thomas E. Starzl** (1926–; see biography in this chapter) attempted the first liver transplant in 1963. Medical professionals were intrigued by his attempt, since at that time there was no treatment for end-stage

American surgeon Joseph Murray, who won the Nobel Prize for medicine or physiology in 1990 for his work in organ transplantation. (Reproduced by permission of the Corbis Corporation.)

liver disease. However, Starzl's patient died shortly after the operation. Not long after that first case, surgeons performed six more liver transplants at three different medical centers. Each patient died within one month of receiving the new liver. Liver transplants were put on hold so that scientists could study the patient's post-operative complications—in particular, their immune system responses.

In 1967, after more potent anti-rejection drugs became available, Starzl's team again attempted a liver transplant. This patient survived for thirteen months. Starzl then began training other surgeons in liver transplant techniques. The procedure rapidly grew in popularity; by the late 1990s,

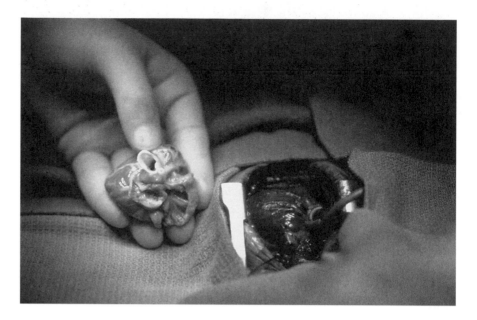

A small, diseased
heart is held next to a
healthy heart.
(Reproduced by
permission of Photo
Researchers, Inc.)

more than 100 medical centers across the United States were performing
liver transplants, and the survival rate after one year was 80 percent.

Heart transplants

The world's first heart transplant was performed in South Africa by surgeon Christiaan Barnard (1922–2001; see box on page 227) on December
3, 1967; the patient survived for eighteen days. The following year surgeons in the United States led by Dr. Norman Shumway (1923–) transplanted a heart into a fifty-four-year-old man; the patient lived for fifteen
days. Around the same time, Dr. Barnard performed his second heart
transplant, after which the patient lived for eighteen months. Several
unsuccessful heart transplants followed in 1968. Heart transplantation
essentially stopped during the 1970s, only to be restarted in 1983 after
cyclosporin and other anti-rejection drugs became available.

By the end of the twentieth century heart transplants had become
commonplace, after one hundred thousand such operations had taken
place around the world. In the United States alone, there were 160 hospitals that carried out the procedure. As the century came to a close, the survival rate for heart recipients after one year was 85 percent to 90 percent
and after five years was 75 percent.

Overcoming shortages with xenotransplantation

At the turn of the twenty-first century, doctors faced an acute shortage of
organs for transplant patients. One response was to experiment with xenotransplantation, the process of transplanting animal organs (primarily

Christiaan Barnard

Christiaan Barnard.
(Reproduced by permission of AP/Wide World Photos.)

South African surgeon Christiaan Barnard (1922–2001) shocked the world on December 3, 1967, by performing the world's first human heart transplant. Barnard replaced the diseased heart of 53-year-old Louis Washkansky, a grocer, with a healthy heart from a brain-dead, twenty-five-year-old female car-crash victim. Although the surgery appeared successful at first, the patient died eighteen days later of pneumonia. Washkansky was at risk for the disease because he had been given large doses of anti-rejection medication, which weakened his immune system.

Barnard performed his second human heart transplant on January 2, 1968. In that case, he not only made medical history but also political history: the donor was a young man of mixed race and the recipient was a retired white dentist, Philip Blaiberg. That action was considered shocking during a time of apartheid (a form of government based on racial segregation and discrimination), when even casual mingling between races was frowned on. Barnard gave Blaiberg smaller doses of immunosuppressant than he had given to Washkansky, and Blaiberg lived for eighteen months after the transplant.

Barnard continued conducting heart transplants and other surgeries until 1983. In that year he was forced to retire after he developed rheumatoid arthritis in his fingers. Barnard spent much of his time thereafter in Austria, writing an autobiography and several novels. He died of an asthma attack at a resort in Cyprus on September 2, 2001.

from pigs) into humans. One famous case of xenotransplantation was the placement of a baboon heart into an infant known as "Baby Fae" in 1984 at the Loma Linda Medical Center in California. The baby's new heart functioned for twenty days.

In July 1996 the Institute of Medicine (a branch of the National Academy of Sciences) published a report that expressed cautious support for xenotransplantation. The institute recognized that the practice may provide a solution to the organ shortage problem but stated a number of concerns. A top concern was the potential for an infection to be carried by the animal organ, which would not only harm the person receiving the organ but might also introduce a new, and potentially deadly, infection into the human population. Research into xenotransplantation continues, and the technique will probably be practiced on a limited basis in the early twenty-first century.

Impact

Organ transplantation has had a tremendous impact on society. First of all, it provides a means of extending the lives of people with fatal organ diseases. The one-year and five-year survival rates for organ recipients are promising, and more than 75 percent of successful transplant recipients return to the lives they enjoyed before they became ill.

There are some causes for concern, however. Transplantation remains risky; between 6 percent and 40 percent (depending on the organ transplanted) of organ recipients die within a year of the operation. In addition, recipients must take medication and undergo frequent examinations for the rest of their lives. For the first few weeks after the operation, when the organ recipient is taking immunosuppressant drugs, they are at risk for a range of diseases and must remain in a sterile (germ-free) room in a hospital. Immunosuppressant drugs have a range of side effects, ranging from hair growth on the face and body to kidney failure.

Deciding who gets the organs

Organ transplantation has raised ethical concerns about the rights of potential organ donors and the distribution of donated organs. Since cyclosporin was introduced and transplant success rates began to rise, the demand for organs has been consistently greater than the supply. Approximately 20,000 organ transplants are performed in the United States each year. At the end of the twentieth century, there were more than 67,000 people in the United States on a waiting list to receive organs and only about 5,000 donors per year. Roughly fifteen people die each day while awaiting organ transplants. That raises the difficult question of how to decide which people should receive the few available organs.

In 1984, the U.S. Congress passed the National Organ Transplantation Act, which set up a centralized system for sharing available organs and a

Liver transplant recipient Jim Pickard holds up an organ donor card. (Reproduced by permission of AP/Wide World Photos.)

scientific register to collect and report transplant information. It also outlawed the sale or purchase of organs. That same year, the United Network for Organ Sharing (UNOS), a nonprofit agency, was created to set up guidelines for deciding which organ recipients should be given a high priority and to match donors with recipients. UNOS works with all transplant centers in the United States to ensure that the limited supply of organs is distributed fairly to patients, regardless of age, gender, race, lifestyle, or economic status. UNOS is guided by the following scientific criteria in choosing who will receive organs: the severity of the patient's disease, the compatibility of blood and tissue types and body size between donor and recipient, and the length of time the recipient has been on the waiting list.

Recruiting organ donors

UNOS and public health organizations have started campaigns to increase the number of people who have agreed to be organ donors. Two obvious measures are the inclusion of organ donor status on driver's licenses and the distribution of a universal donor card that indicates the bearers' desire to donate their organs upon their death. In 1981 the federal government ruled that it was legal to remove organs from a willing patient once that person was declared brain dead. During the 1980s and 1990s, most states passed laws requiring medical personnel to ask all potential donor patients or their families (if the patient was unable to respond) to decide whether they would donate their organs. Officials of all major religions in the United States have declared their support for the campaign to raise public awareness of organ donation.

Ethical concerns about organ donation

Even with these efforts to recruit organ donors, demand for organs continues to increase faster than the supply. The desperate need for more organs has raised ethical concerns regarding the sources of donated organs and the rights of potential organ donors. Some people question whether every effort is made to save a dying person who is a potential organ donor, especially when there is pressure on doctors to produce organs for transplantation. There have also been reports that people have sold their own organs for financial gain and that organized crime groups have become involved in buying and selling organs.

☐ THE AIDS PANDEMIC

Overview

AIDS, which stands for "acquired immunodeficiency syndrome," is a disease caused by the human immunodeficiency virus (HIV). HIV works by weakening the patient's immune system, leaving the body unable to fight off a wide range of illnesses.

HIV is transmitted through bodily fluids: blood, semen, vaginal fluids, and breast milk. The virus cannot be transmitted by sneezing or coughing or through casual physical contact. It can only be transmitted by activities such as sexual intercourse, sharing hypodermic needles, and breastfeeding.

The U.S. Centers for Disease Control (CDC) officially recognized AIDS as a disease in 1981. Since that time, according to statistics from the United Nations, AIDS has killed an estimated 22 million people worldwide, 80 percent of them in Africa. In the fall of 2001, the number of people globally living with HIV or AIDS was estimated at 40 million. AIDS is considered a "pandemic," meaning it is a health crisis of worldwide proportions. (An epidemic, in contrast, affects a large number of people in a particular area or areas.)

In the 1990s researchers developed numerous drugs to slow the advance of AIDS; at the beginning of the twenty-first century, health advocates were working to lower the price of the drugs and make them available to people in poor countries. Medical officials were also in pursuit of a vaccine that would prevent healthy people from getting AIDS. As a result of these new treatments, health workers noted the American public was growing less worried about the dangers of AIDS, and they warned that such an attitude could result in more people being infected with HIV.

Background

By 1981, when the CDC officially recognized AIDS as a disease, it had been seeing clusters of rare illnesses, such as *Pneumocystis carinii* pneumo-

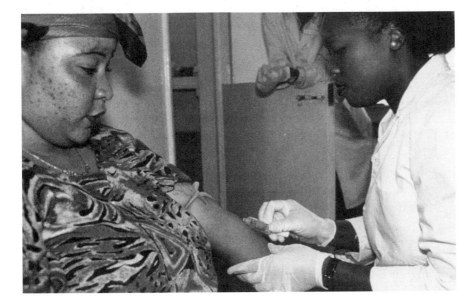

Nurse drawing blood from an HIV-resistant prostitute at Majengo Clinic in Nairobi, Kenya. (Reproduced by permission of Photo Researchers, Inc.)

nia (PCP) and Kaposi's sarcoma (a type of cancer) in previously healthy homosexual men in New York and California. Both diseases tend to arise in individuals with severely crippled immune systems.

By the end of the year 2000, AIDS had killed nearly 450,000 Americans, out of nearly 750,000 U.S. residents who had been infected with HIV. The number of new AIDS cases diagnosed in the U.S. decreased in 1996 for the first time since 1981; that decline continued through 1998. Deaths due to AIDS also dropped to about 16,000 in 1998. This was largely due to educational campaigns about how AIDS is spread and how to practice "safe sex," coupled with effective new drug treatments. In the year 2001, however, authorities sounded the alarm that the decline in AIDS cases had leveled off since 1998.

The spread of AIDS worldwide

In recent years, the incidence of AIDS worldwide has been increasing at an alarming rate, affecting people in Africa, South America, Asia, and Western Europe. Studies published by the World Health Organization (WHO) indicated that within ten years of the discovery of AIDS, 5 million to 10 million people around the world had been infected with HIV, and since the early 1980s, more than 22 million people had died of AIDS.

Today, roughly 70 percent of the world's HIV-infected people live in Africa. Most of them are in sub-Saharan Africa (the portion of Africa south of the Sahara Desert, including Kenya, Ethiopia, Uganda, and Tanzania). In the countries of Botswana and Zimbabwe, more than 25 percent of the

acquired immunodeficiency syndrome: also called AIDS; a disease caused by the human immunodeficiency virus (HIV) that weakens the patient's immune system.

AIDS cocktail: a treatment for AIDS consisting of azidothymidine (also called zidovudine or AZT), lamivudine (3TC), and a protease inhibitor (which works by blocking another enzyme, called protease, that helps the virus replicate in the host cell) such as indinavir or saquinavir.

human immunodeficiency virus: also called HIV; an unusual form of virus, called a retrovirus, that causes AIDS.

Kaposi's sarcoma: a malignant skin cancer characterized by blue-red flat or raised blotches on the limbs and body.

opportunistic infections: infections that take advantage of a weakened immune system.

pneumocystis carinii pneumonia: also called PCP; a common lung infection in AIDS patients.

progressive multifocal leukoencephalopathy: also called PML; a central nervous system disease that causes gradual brain degeneration.

adult population has HIV or AIDS. In contrast with the United States, where the majority of AIDS victims have been homosexual men, AIDS in Africa was first recognized in heterosexuals and has affected women and men in equal numbers.

In Asia, India has the most AIDS cases. The Chinese government recently revealed that growing numbers of Chinese are infected with HIV; some experts predict that 10 million Chinese citizens could have the virus by the year 2010, the largest number of any country in the world. AIDS is also a growing problem in Eastern Europe and the former Soviet Union. Making matters worse, many infected people in poor countries cannot afford even basic medical treatment for the disease.

Identification of the virus

HIV was discovered in 1984 by American researcher **Robert Gallo** (1937–; see biography in this chapter), working at the National Institutes of Health in Maryland, and French virologist (a scientist who studies viruses) Luc Montagnier (1932–), at the Pasteur Institute in Paris. That same year Gallo developed a blood test to detect the presence of HIV. Tests conducted on stored blood samples indicated that HIV first appeared in the United States in the late 1970s.

Transmission of HIV and development of AIDS

HIV is an unusual form of virus called a retrovirus, and it is more difficult to treat than other viruses that affect humans. The genetic material that makes up a typical virus is DNA (deoxyribonucleic acid; complex molecules that carry genetic information). However, the genetic material that makes up a retrovirus is RNA (ribonucleic acid). When a retrovirus invades a cell (known as a host cell), its RNA converts to DNA through an enzyme called reverse transcriptase. As a result, the retrovirus combines with and takes over the DNA of the host cell. HIV replicates (copies itself) so rapidly that several billion new virus particles can be produced every day.

Luc Montagnier, the French virologist and professor who discovered the AIDS virus. (Reproduced by permission of AP/Wide World Photos.)

The period between the time a person is infected with HIV and the time they develop full-blown AIDS ranges from two to twelve years, with an average of eight years between infection and onset. For the first few years after infection, the patient may look and feel completely healthy. The infected person may then develop symptoms such as night sweats, fevers, weight loss, diarrhea, skin rash, coughing, and shortness of breath. For unknown reasons, HIV goes through periods of activity and dormancy (a resting state) in the body. When HIV is active, it infects and kills certain white blood cells, called helper T cells, which are an important part of the immune system. HIV also infects brain cells and immune-system cells called macrophages.

Once the disease progresses to full-blown AIDS, the patient may suffer a number of opportunistic infections (infections that take advantage of a weakened immune system). Examples include herpes viruses, oral thrush (which is caused by the fungus *candida albicans*), *Pneumocystis carinii* pneumonia (PCP, a common lung infection in AIDS patients), and progressive multifocal leukoencephalopathy (PML, a central nervous system disease that causes gradual brain degeneration). Many AIDS patients develop Kaposi's sarcoma, which is a malignant skin cancer characterized by blue-red flat or raised blotches on the limbs and body.

Development of AIDS treatments

When AIDS was first recognized in 1981, patients who developed full-blown AIDS could expect to die within a year or two. Even as late as 1996, more than 75 percent of patients diagnosed with AIDS would die within two years. In the late 1990s, however, researchers developed powerful drugs that, taken in combination, promised to prolong the life of a person with AIDS for several years. These drugs seek to prevent the virus from reproducing without damaging the host cells.

The most promising AIDS treatment is a combination of three drugs, often referred to as the AIDS "cocktail." The trio consists of azidothymidine (also called zidovudine or AZT), lamivudine (3TC), and a protease inhibitor (which works by blocking another enzyme, called protease, that helps the virus replicate in the host cell) such as indinavir or saquinavir. One drawback to the cocktail is that patients must take fourteen to twenty pills a day on a strict schedule.

In many patients who have taken the cocktail correctly, HIV levels in the bloodstream have been reduced to undetectable levels. Studies done in 2001, however, found that the drugs did not eliminate the virus; when patients stopped taking the drug combinations, HIV came back at very high levels.

Efforts to find a vaccine

Throughout the 1990s and into the early twenty-first century, AIDS researchers worked to create a vaccine that would prevent people from being infected with HIV. Despite many promising developments, however, scientists were unable to produce an effective vaccine. HIV is difficult to deal with because it merges with host cells in a way that makes it almost unrecognizable by antibodies. (Antibodies are agents created in response to a vaccine that recognize and attack a particular infection.) HIV is also hard for antibodies to detect because it goes through frequent genetic changes.

In the fall of 2001, Robert Gallo, the co-discoverer of HIV, announced that he had produced a vaccine that showed success in tests on macaque monkeys. The vaccine was able to produce antibodies that attacked a variety of HIV strains from around the world. At the end of that year, Gallo and other researchers were preparing to test the vaccine on human subjects.

Activists from the group Act Up staging a "Die-In" in front of St. Patrick's Cathedral in New York City, 1994.
(Reproduced by permission of Archive Photos, Inc.)

Impact

The spread of AIDS has posed many social and ethical dilemmas. Because AIDS first affected primarily homosexual males in the United States (although poor African American women later became at high risk for the disease as well), it was labeled a "gay" disease. Many social critics believed that widespread homophobia (fear of homosexuals) in American society prevented AIDS researchers from getting the support and funding they needed. Some religious leaders expressed the opinion that AIDS was God's punishment for homosexuality, and that gay men had somehow brought the disease on themselves. Furthermore, the association of AIDS with poverty, substance abuse, prostitution, and homelessness has made the disease a topic that many Americans would prefer to ignore.

The controversy over AIDS research spending and homophobia sparked an AIDS protest movement among the gay and lesbian community. Since the late 1980s, AIDS advocacy groups have loudly demanded increased funding for AIDS research and fought for the rights of people with AIDS, as well as opposing anti-gay violence and discrimination. The most visible AIDS activist group, ACT UP (which stands for AIDS Coalition to Unleash Power) uses street theater and civil disobedience to draw attention to its cause.

Cost of treatment

One reason AIDS has taken such a huge toll on developing nations is that the cost of AIDS drugs—and even basic health care—is incredibly expensive. In the spring of 2001 the price of the life-saving (or at least life-extending) drugs was the focus of international legal action. The result was that western manufacturers agreed to give up their patents and allow generic forms of the drugs to be distributed in poor nations. The generic drugs would cost a patient about $350 per year, as opposed to the $15,000 to $20,000 per year for the non-generic versions. While even that cost was more than many people with AIDS in developing nations could afford, it meant that governments and international health agencies could purchase large quantities of the generic drugs to distribute at little or no cost to AIDS patients.

☐ THE DEVELOPMENT OF HIGH-TECH MEDICAL DIAGNOSTIC TOOLS

Overview

In the latter part of the twentieth century, high-tech devices that can see inside the body became powerful diagnostic tools (tools that can identify a disease). Using these imaging (picture-producing) tools, doctors are able to explore parts and functions of the body without using surgery. The advances in imaging technology, which mostly occurred in the 1970s, were a direct result of the growth in computer capabilities as well as developments in physics and mathematics. Although the various types of imaging equipment use different techniques (for example, electromagnetism and sound waves), all rely on computers to interpret the signals and construct visual images. With high-tech imaging equipment, diagnosing disorders in the human body has become more accurate, safer, and more economical.

Background

The first device used to look inside the body and photograph bones and internal organs was the X-ray machine. X rays are a form of electromagnetic radiation (radiation that transmits energy through the interaction of electricity and magnetism) with a wavelength about 1,000 times shorter than that of visible light. X rays travel through solid substances with low densities but are reflected or absorbed by high-density materials. X rays are commonly used to identify broken bones and diseases of the major organs.

The development of X-ray machines has its roots in the research of German physicist Wilhelm Roentgen (1845–1923). In 1895 Roentgen experimented with a cathode-ray tube, a tube through which electrons are rapidly scanned, creating patterns of moving light on a fluorescent screen. He determined that the tube gave off invisible rays, which were later identified as X rays, that could pass through wood and paper and light up a fluorescent screen several yards away. When Roentgen aimed the cathode-ray tube at his hand, an image of his bones appeared on the fluorescent screen.

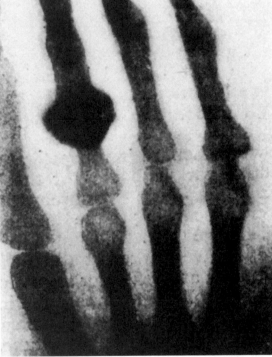

The first X-ray tube (called the Coolidge tube) designed specifically for medical use was invented by American chemist William Coolidge (1873–1975) in 1913. X-ray devices were widely used to treat soldiers during World War II (1939–45).

Modern X-ray machines are far more efficient than the early versions, requiring just milliseconds of exposure to produce an image. Since we now know that overexposure to X rays can cause cancer, this has made X-ray imaging far safer. Modern X-ray machines also create images in far greater detail, and instead of producing an image on a fluorescent screen or photographic plate, they create a digital picture that can be processed and stored on a computer.

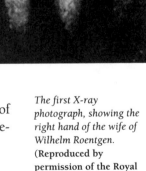

The first X-ray photograph, showing the right hand of the wife of Wilhelm Roentgen. (Reproduced by permission of the Royal Institute of Technology.)

Computed tomography (CT) scanning

During the late 1960s, improved computer capabilities made possible the development of computed tomography (CT) scanning, also known as computer-assisted tomography or computerized axial tomography (CAT) scanning. The word "tomography" comes from the Greek word *tomos*, meaning "section"; tomography is the X-ray photography of a selected

computed tomography (CT) scanning: an X-ray technique in which a three-dimensional image of a body part is put together by computer using a series of X-ray pictures taken from different angles along a straight line; often called computerized axial tomography (CAT).

diagnostic: pertaining to the identification of a diseased condition.

magnetic resonance imaging (MRI): the process of subjecting a sample of material to a strong magnetic field and radio waves and observing the response of the atoms in that sample; it is used to produce detailed, three-dimensional computer images of body tissues and organs.

mammography: X-ray visualization of breast tissue.

nuclear magnetic resonance (NMR): the application of radio waves to samples of certain elements in the presence of a strong magnetic field. This causes the nuclei to spin at a particular frequency and can be used to determine the structure of molecules. Its medical application is called magnetic resonance imaging.

ultrasound: a technique that uses high-frequency sound waves—beyond the range that humans can hear—to see inside the body; also called ultrasonics or ultrasonography.

X ray: a form of electromagnetic radiation (radiation that transmits energy through the interaction of electricity and magnetism) with a wavelength about 1,000 times shorter than visible light.

plane, or section, of the body. CT scanning produces a three-dimensional, detailed image of the brain and other internal organs. Two scientists independently developed the process in the late 1960s: American physicist Allan Cormack (1924–1998) and English electrical engineer Godfrey Hounsfield (1919–). Cormack and Hounsfield shared the Nobel Prize in physiology or medicine in 1979 for their work.

A CT scanner takes X rays of the brain from many different angles. The X rays are reflected to an electronic detector that sends signals to a powerful computer. Using a series of advanced mathematical processes, the computer combines all of the X-ray data to construct a detailed, three-dimensional image of the brain. That image appears almost immediately on a monitor and is stored on a computer disk. Over the years, CT scanning has been improved to use lower doses of radiation and shorter exposure times. The procedure is a very effective and widely used diagnostic tool that can locate hard-to-find tumors, blood clots, and other disorders of the brain.

Ultrasound devices

The next development in medical imaging technology was ultrasound (also called ultrasonics or ultrasonography). Ultrasound is a technique that uses high-frequency sound waves—beyond the range that humans can hear—to see inside the body. Ultrasonography emerged from techniques developed by the British Royal Air Force during World War II, namely radar (the use of radio waves to determine an object's position) and sonar (the use of sound waves to determine an object's position).

Research into creating an ultrasound device for medical use began in the early 1950s. The first such tool was tested on a human subject in 1957 and successfully diagnosed the patient's heart condition. The following year doctors began to use ultrasound to monitor the condition of a fetus inside the womb. By the 1980s physicians routinely used ultrasound devices on pregnant women.

Today ultrasound is also used to examine delicate organs such as the heart, lungs, liver, eyes, and kidneys, which could be damaged by X rays. In addition to traditional ultrasound machines, there are ultrasonic Doppler devices that can measure the change in the frequency of waves emitted by a moving source. These devices identify ailments related to blood flow (such as arteriosclerosis, or clogging of the arteries) and heart valve defects. Another development late in the twentieth century was the invention of microscopes that use ultrasound to examine cell structures without having to stain them, which is a process that causes the death of the cells. Ultrasonics is the least expensive of all high-tech diagnostic imaging techniques.

Wilhelm Roentgen received the first Nobel Prize in physics in 1901 for the discovery of X rays. (**Reproduced by permission of Archive Photos, Inc.**)

Nuclear magnetic resonance

Another high-tech imaging technique, which was first used for medical diagnosis in the late 1960s, is nuclear magnetic resonance (NMR). NMR produces pictures of bones, tissues, and organs, as well as the structures of large molecules and compounds, by subjecting atoms to a strong magnetic field and radio waves and observing the atoms' response.

Austrian-American physicist Isidor Isaac Rabi (1898–1988) began research into NMR in the late 1930s. Rabi sent a beam of vaporized (converted to a gaseous state) silver through a magnetic field and observed that the nuclei within the silver atoms spun like tops. His research showed that, for nearly every chemical element, the atomic nuclei behave in unique ways when exposed to a magnetic field.

In the mid-1940s two scientists working independently improved the NMR technique: American physicist Edward Mills Purcell (1912–1997) and Swiss-born American physicist Felix Bloch (1905–1983). In the improved process, the substance to be analyzed was placed in the field of a strong electromagnet (a device that becomes magnetized when activated

Patient lying on a mobile table, entering a Computed Tomography (CT) scanner. (Reproduced by permission of Photo Researchers, Inc.)

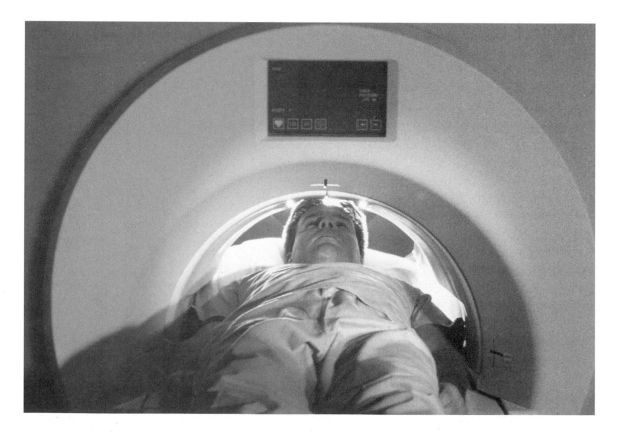

by electrical impulses). A second magnet powered by radio waves was then directed at the substance. The frequency of the radio waves was adjusted until the atoms in the sample vibrated at their maximum frequency, called the sample's "signature frequency." From the signature frequency, a researcher could determine the composition of unidentified chemical samples. Purcell and Bloch shared the 1952 Nobel Prize in physics for their accomplishments.

In the 1960s, American physicist Raymond V. Damadian (1936–) tested the technique on animals. He found that NMR was safe and effective at detecting diseased cells (such as cancer cells) within the body, based on their known signature frequencies.

Magnetic resonance imaging

In the early 1970s, the medical community decided to change the name of the NMR process to magnetic resonance imaging (MRI). This change was made because some patients feared that NMR was associated with nuclear fission or fusion (the splitting and combining of nuclei, respectively)—which, in fact, it was not.

A modern MRI scanner consists of a large, tube-shaped magnet, radio transmitters and receivers, and a computer. While the patient lies inside the tube, an intense magnetic field is created there, causing the nuclei of certain atoms within the patient's body to spin and wobble at precise frequencies. Radio signals are then directed at the patient, at the same frequency as the signature frequency of the type of cells being targeted. When the radio signals and magnetic field are turned off, the nuclei emit bursts of energy absorbed from the radio waves. The computer records these energy bursts and translates their pattern, creating a three-dimensional image of the scanned area.

The medical community was widely using MRI by the mid-1980s, and it remained the most powerful diagnostic tool available at the end of the twentieth century. MRI is especially useful for detecting cancer and for identifying diseases and injuries in the head, spinal cord, chest, joints, bladder, and circulatory system. Due to the high cost of MRI equipment, it is available only in large, state-of-the-art medical centers.

Impact

The development of noninvasive diagnostic techniques (which do not require physically entering the body) has allowed physicians to quickly, safely, and accurately identify illnesses and injuries in patients. These tools also aid surgeons in the operating room by helping them pinpoint the location of tumors, lesions (wounds or abnormal structural changes), and vascular (pertaining to blood or lymph systems) abnormalities. The sur-

Medicine

ESSAYS

geon can then cut into the body at the precise location required. In the 1990s, the combination of information technology (including the Internet) with high-tech diagnostic tools allowed physicians to share data with and seek advice from colleagues in locations around the world.

Mammography reduces breast cancer deaths

Mammography—the X-ray visualization of breast tissue—is one example of a life-saving diagnostic imaging procedure. Mammography was first used in the 1960s, when physicians demonstrated its effectiveness in the early diagnosis of breast cancer. The Breast Cancer Detection Demonstration Project, a five-year study of more than 250,000 women that ended in 1973, helped establish mammography as an effective screening tool for breast cancer. Since that time, mammography has been recommended as part of the yearly checkup for women over the age of 50.

At present, approximately one in nine women develop breast cancer in their lifetime. Yearly screening increases a woman's chance of detecting breast cancer in its earliest stages, when tumors are small and most easily treated. Eighty-two percent of women whose breast cancer is caught in the early stages survive for five years. In contrast, when breast cancer is not diagnosed until a later stage, patients have a five-year survival rate of just 60 percent.

☐ ADVANCES IN UNDERSTANDING CANCER

Overview

Cancer is a group of more than one hundred diseases characterized by the uncontrolled multiplication of abnormal cells within the body. Cancer cells are abnormal in that they have chromosomes (structures that organize genetic information in the nucleus of a cell) with genes that are missing or in a different location. Cancer cells can form tumors (swollen parts or growths) that crowd out and destroy nearby tissues. They can also metastasize, or shed cells that develop into tumors at other locations in the body. If cancer cells enter a vital organ such as the liver or kidneys, they can prevent that organ from functioning and kill the patient.

By the second half of the twentieth century, cancer—along with heart disease and stroke—had replaced infectious, epidemic diseases (diseases with a rapid increase in the rate of infection) as the leading causes of death in the United States. Although cancer has been around for centuries, only in the late twentieth century did scientists begin to understand the causes of cancer and develop effective treatments. Many new methods of cancer treatment remained experimental at the end of the twentieth century.

Words to Know

cancer: a disease characterized by the uncontrolled multiplication of abnormal cells within the body.

carcinogen: a substance that causes cancer.

chemotherapy: the use of powerful chemicals to kill cancer cells in the human body.

gene therapy: an experimental technique involving altering human genes to cure certain genetic disorders.

radiotherapy: the use of radiation to shrink cancerous tumors.

tumor: a swollen part or growth.

Although a cure for cancer is still unavailable, a variety of therapies aimed at shrinking tumors and killing cancer cells have significantly increased the survival rates of cancer patients. In the 1940s, only one in four cancer patients survived five years or more after beginning treatment; in the year 2000 the five-year survival rate was 60 percent. And in the 1990s, for the first time in more than seventy years, the overall death rate due to cancer in the United States dropped. This achievement was attributed to lower levels of cigarette smoking coupled with aggressive new medical treatments.

Background

In centuries past, scientists had little understanding of the nature, causes, or treatments of cancer. It was once thought, for instance, that people who developed cancer had "unbalanced humors" (insanity or bad character). As early as the eighteenth century, when chimney sweeps (people who cleaned soot and ash from chimneys) developed a high rate of cancer of the scrotum, scientists suspected a connection between certain chemicals and cancer. Since that time, many other potential causes of cancer have surfaced.

Causes of cancer

In recent years, scientists have suggested the following factors—acting alone or in combination—as causing cancer: diets rich in fat or sugar, the

Heads of the nation's largest cigarette companies being sworn in before a hearing of a House Energy subcommittee on Capitol Hill, 1994. (Reproduced by permission of AP/Wide World Photos.)

accumulation of metabolic toxins (waste products) in the body, aging, hormonal imbalances, infection by parasites, viruses, excessive alcohol consumption, genetic predisposition (having genes with cells that are more likely to become cancerous), overhead power lines, tobacco, X rays, radioactive fallout (radioactive debris that is sent into the air after a nuclear explosion), ultraviolet radiation (from sunlight), depression, stress, carcinogens (cancer-causing agents) that occur naturally in foods, radon gas, and even cell phones. It is also possible that chemicals used in agriculture and industry cause cancer (for a discussion of those factors, see the section "The environmental factor" on page 248).

There are more than twenty-four viruses that are known to cause cancer in humans. The hepatitis B virus, for instance, can cause liver cancer. Exposure to the rare Epstein-Barr virus can bring on Burkitt's lymphoma, a tumor that often affects the jaw and digestive system. The human papilloma virus (a genital herpes virus) makes women more likely to develop cancer of the cervix. And the human immunodeficiency virus (HIV, the virus that causes AIDS) produces Kaposi's sarcoma, a skin cancer characterized by blue-red flat or raised blotches on the limbs and body (see essay The AIDS Pandemic in this chapter).

The tobacco-cancer connection

Cigarettes and other tobacco products were first conclusively linked to lung cancer in 1964, in a landmark report by Surgeon General Luther Terry titled *Smoking and Health: Report of the Advisory Committee to the*

Surgeon General of the Public Health Service. Studies over the past three decades have strengthened the link between cigarette smoking and cancer. At present, about 30 percent of cancer deaths in the United States are related to tobacco products.

In 1997, a cigarette manufacturer called the Liggett Group admitted that for thirty years the tobacco industry had known about and concealed the dangers of cigarettes. The corporation also revealed that cigarette companies adjusted levels of nicotine (the addictive substance in tobacco) in cigarettes in order to make them more addictive. Furthermore, the Liggett Group reported, cigarette companies added ammonia to tobacco, which changed the structure of nicotine so lung tissue would absorb it more quickly.

In 1997 the U.S. Food and Drug Administration (FDA) won the legal right to regulate cigarettes and smokeless tobacco products (such as chewing tobacco) as "drug delivery devices." As a result, children under age 18 are banned from buying cigarettes, cigarette package warning labels use stronger language, and a nationwide public education campaign has emphasized the health hazards of smoking to the public.

The percentage of adults in the United States who smoke fell sharply between 1965 and 1990, from 42 to 25 percent. Between 1990 and 1998,

Anti-smoking advertisement aimed at children. (Reproduced by permission of AP/Wide World Photos.)

however, the rate remained almost unchanged. Another disturbing trend in the 1990s was that cigarette smoking among high school students increased from 28 to 35 percent.

Treatments

One of the oldest techniques used to treat cancer, which was mentioned in the notes of the ancient Greek physician Hippocrates (c. 460–c. 377 B.C.E.), known as the "father of medicine," is surgery. As Hippocrates observed, however, such operations rarely cured the patient. Even today, surgery is successful only in certain cases, such as if the cancer is in its early stages and the growth of abnormal cells is limited to one area in the body. For instance, if a tumor exists in a portion of the colon, lung, or breast, surgeons may remove that tissue. Even in those cases, however, surgery will cure the patient only if all of the cancer cells are removed, which is not always possible.

In recent decades, doctors have developed alternative cancer treatments that are used in combination with surgery or with each other. The most common treatments are chemotherapy (the use of chemical medications), and radiotherapy (the use of radiation to shrink cancerous tumors). Chemotherapy, which is the main treatment for several types of cancer, traces its origins to mustard gas used during World War I (1914–18). Autopsies of soldiers killed by mustard gas showed that the gas had stopped their white blood cells from reproducing. This was important because cancer cells divide at a faster rate than normal cells, and doctors were searching for an agent that would stop them from reproducing. At the beginning of the twenty-first century, doctors had a variety of drugs and hormones that could stop cancer cells from reproducing by destroying the genetic material in those cells.

Chemotherapy is often combined with radiotherapy. Unfortunately, both treatments kill healthy cells along with cancer cells. Chemotherapy and radiotherapy also have serious side effects, such as severe nausea and loss of hair.

Gene-based approaches

The malfunction of genes that control cell growth and division is at the root of every case of cancer. About 5 percent to 10 percent of cancer cases are hereditary—that is, the cancer is caused by defective genes that the patient inherited from one or both parents. Health professionals are attempting to prevent hereditary cancer by identifying which genes are linked to tumors through genetic fingerprinting, the process that maps out a person's unique sequence of DNA (deoxyribonucleic acid; complex molecules that carry genetic information). The next step is to treat the abnormal gene using gene therapy, a new and experimental technique in which a doctor alters human genes to cure certain genetic disorders (inherited diseases caused by a tiny change in a single gene).

Throughout the 1990s, scientists experimented with gene therapy in attempts to cure skin cancer along with many other diseases. They are also making progress in finding genetic markers (a gene or trait that can be used to identify genes and traits that are linked to it) and mutations (changes) that seem to make people more likely to develop certain cancers. Genetic research, for instance, has identified the precise genes that are linked to breast cancer. Women who have flaws in one of these genes (which can be detected with a blood test) have a 55 percent to 85 percent likelihood of developing breast cancer. Researchers have suggested that these women undergo annual breast cancer tests called mammograms (see essay The Development of High-Tech Medical Diagnostic Tools in this chapter) beginning at age twenty-five (as opposed to the usual age of fifty) and take other measures to guard against breast cancer.

Impact

Today, one in three people in developed countries will develop cancer at some point in their lifetime. In the United States, one of every four deaths is from cancer. According to the American Cancer Society, nearly 13 million new cancer cases were diagnosed in the United States between 1990 and 2000, and more than 1,500 Americans die of cancer each day. Cancer is the second leading cause of death in the United States (heart disease is first). Despite billions of dollars spent on research and efforts by health professionals, there is as yet no cure or vaccine for cancer.

Until a vaccine or a cure is developed, there are certain steps you can take to reduce your chances of developing cancer: don't smoke; eat a diet high in fruits, vegetables, and whole grains and low in fat; avoid contact with materials such as asbestos and PCBs (polychlorinated biphenyls; chemicals used in manufacturing); have your home tested for radon; eat organic produce (fruits and vegetables that have not been sprayed with pesticides); maintain a healthy weight; and engage in moderate exercise for at least thirty minutes every day.

The "War on Cancer"

In 1937, the U.S. government created the National Cancer Institute (NCI) as a division of the National Institutes of Health (NIH) to conduct a "war on cancer." At that time the disease was seen as a plague that threatened the existence of the human race. In 1971, by which time there had been little progress in finding effective treatments for cancer, the U.S. Congress passed the Cancer Act. That legislation supplied $1.5 billion for cancer research and created a National Cancer Advisory Board that reported to the

Aerosol sprays are powered by chemicals called chlorofluorocarbons (CFCs). CFCs and other pollutants in the air contribute to the thinning of the ozone layer. (Reproduced by permission of Sinclair Stammers/Science Photo Library.)

president. While the success of the "war on cancer" in the 1970s was questionable, the advances made in understanding the origins of cancer made it possible for researchers to develop life-extending therapies in later decades.

The environmental factor

The possibility that some cancers are caused by human-made toxins or conditions in the environment received a great deal of attention toward the end of the twentieth century. One example of a cancerous agent in the environment is the pesticide dichlorodiphenyltrichloroethane (better known as DDT), which in large doses can cause liver cancer and other diseases. (Pesticides are chemicals applied to crops to kill insect pests and weeds.) The United States banned DDT in 1972; however, it is still widely used in other parts of the world. Also linked to some forms of cancer in humans, as well as miscarriages and birth defects, are the herbicides (chemicals that kill weeds) 2,4-D and 2,4,5-T. The United States banned 2,4,5-T in 1979 but still allows the use of 2,4-D.

The increase in cases of skin cancer, which is caused by exposure to ultraviolet radiation, has been linked to the destruction of the ozone layer (the atmospheric layer that absorbs ultraviolet rays from the sun). Chlorofluorocarbons (CFCs; chemicals used in aerosol spray cans and foam-blowing canisters) and other pollutants in the air contribute to the thinning of the ozone layer. It is estimated that a 1 percent reduction in the ozone layer results in a 2 percent to 5 percent rise in the incidence of skin cancer. Some cases of cancer in city dwellers may be caused by compounds in the exhaust produced by cars and factory smokestacks, especially the carcinogenic substances benzene and benzopyrene.

◻ ALEXIS CARREL (1873–1944)

French physician and surgeon

Carrel is best known for developing surgical techniques that doctors later used to transplant organs. In 1912 he won the Nobel Prize in physiology or medicine for his method of sewing together the ends of very small blood vessels using tiny needles and extremely fine thread. In Carrel's later years he became controversial for his support of selectively breeding "superior" individuals in order to improve the human race.

Experiments with repairing blood vessels

Carrel was born just outside Lyons, France, on June 28, 1873. His father, a silk merchant, died when Carrel was very young. Carrel received much of his early education at home, taught by his mother. When he came of age he attended the University of Lyons, completing a bachelor of arts degree in 1889 and bachelor of science degree in 1890. He earned his medical degree from the same university in 1900. Carrel then practiced medicine at the Lyons Hospital; he also taught anatomy and operative surgery at the university.

Alexis Carrel.
(Courtesy of the
Library of Congress.)

The direction of Carrel's medical career was influenced by the 1894 death of the French president, who was stabbed by an assassin in Lyons. Had there been a method for repairing blood vessels, Carrel believed, the president might have survived. Early in his medical career Carrel began searching for such a method; he experimented by sewing with very fine silk thread on paper. He also researched ways to keep cells around the broken blood vessels alive. In 1902 Carrel published a paper on his methods of sewing together tiny blood vessels, but it received little attention.

Keeps heart tissue alive

In 1904 Carrel moved to the United States and spent two years in the department of physiology at the University of Chicago. There he used his experimental methods to perform organ transplants on animals. While the transplants at first appeared to be successful, within minutes or days of the operation the organs would fail and the animals would die. (At that time scientists had not yet learned to overcome organ rejection by the body's immune system; see essay The Development of Organ Transplantation in this chapter.)

In 1906 Carrel became an associate member of the Rockefeller Institute for Medical Research (now Rockefeller University) in New York City; he became a full member in 1912. It was there that Carrel continued to perfect his technique for suturing (sewing together) blood vessels that won him a Nobel Prize in physiology or medicine in 1912.

Carrel also believed that someday blood transfusions and organ transplants would be possible. In 1912, he showed that blood vessels in organs or tissue could be preserved, at low temperatures, for long periods of time, which would make it possible to save organs for transplant. In one case, he kept alive heart tissue from a chick embryo in a dish in the laboratory. The tissue outlived Carrel, surviving for thirty-four years until it was intentionally destroyed.

Military service

During World War I (1914–18) Carrel served in the French Army Medical Corps. There he helped create the Carrel-Dakin method of treating war wounds, which involved cleaning wounds with sodium hypochlorite to fight infection. Although the practice was widely used at the time, doctors discontinued it after antibiotics became available during World War II (1939–45; see essay The Discovery, Importance, and Limitations of Antibiotics in this chapter). After his military service ended, Carrel returned to the Rockefeller Institute and turned his attention to finding the causes of cancer.

Designs organ-preservation machine

In the early 1930s, still concentrating on keeping organs alive outside the body, Carrel worked with American aviator Charles Lindbergh (1902–1974) to build the first version of a mechanical heart. (Lindbergh had become interested in the problem when his sister-in-law developed a heart condition.) The device was a special pump made of glass that would circulate germ-free nutrient fluids and maintain organs in the laboratory. Carrel and Lindbergh appeared together with their device, called a "perfusion pump," in the June 13, 1938, issue of *Time* magazine. They also co-wrote the 1938 book *The Culture of Organs,* in which they described the workings of the machine and its usefulness for organ transplantation.

Views provoke controversy

Also in the early 1930s Carrel was at work on a book that brought together his views on philosophy, religion, politics, and science. Titled *Man, the Unknown* and published in 1935, the controversial, best-selling book presented Carrel's idea that humankind could reach perfection by selectively breeding "superior" individuals and argued that intellectuals should govern society. Among those who were opposed to Carrel's views as being anti-democratic was the director of the Rockefeller Institute. The director canceled Carrel's program—the division of experimental surgery—and put pressure on Carrel to retire.

In 1941 Carrel returned to his native France, which had been conquered by German dictator Adolf Hitler (1885–1945). Carrel accepted a position with the Foundation for the Study of Human Problems, an agency of the new French government established by the Germans. In 1944, when the Germans were driven from France, the new French government accused Carrel of having helped the Nazis. Before Carrel could stand trial, however, he died of a heart attack on November 5, 1944.

◘ BENJAMIN CARSON (1951–)

American neurosurgeon

Benjamin Carson made medical history in 1987 when he successfully separated a pair of Siamese twins joined at the head. Carson had become famous two years earlier, when he performed a hemispherectomy—removal of half the brain—on a young girl, curing her of terrible seizures. Also in the mid-1980s, Carson conducted groundbreaking surgery on a fetus while it was still in its mother's womb. The fetus, one of a set of twins, had hydrocephaly (fluid on the brain), which caused an abnormal swelling of its head. Carson removed the extra fluid and relieved the swelling.

Benjamin Carson. (Reproduced by permission of Richard T. Nowitz/Photo Researchers, Inc.)

A turbulent beginning

Carson was born on September 18, 1951, in Detroit, Michigan. His father abandoned the family when Carson was eight years old, leaving his mother, a domestic worker, to support Carson and his brother. As a child, Carson did badly at school and frequently got into fights. He credits his mother with saving him from failure; starting when he was ten years old, she made him read two books a week and forbade him to watch television. Carson's hard work paid off, and he graduated at the top of his high school class.

Carson then received a scholarship to Yale University and completed his undergraduate education there in 1973. He next enrolled in the school of medicine at the University of Michigan in Ann Arbor. While a medical student he married Lacena Rustin (nicknamed "Candy"), a classmate from Yale; they eventually had three children.

In 1977 Carson earned his medical degree. He and his wife moved to Baltimore, Maryland, so that Carson could do his internship at Johns Hopkins University. Within five years, Carson—the hospital's first African American neurosurgery (surgery of nerve tissue) resident—had been named the chief resident of neurosurgery.

Begins career in neurosurgery

In 1983 Carson traveled to Perth, Australia, to gain experience in brain surgery at the Sir Charles Gairdner Hospital. The following year he returned to Johns Hopkins and became the director of pediatric (children's) neurosurgery. In 1985 Carson performed his first landmark operation, a hemispherectomy, on an eighteen-month-old girl who suffered from 100 or more seizures per day. The operation cured the girl's condition. Carson has since completed many other hemispherectomies.

Carson gained international fame in 1987, when he headed a team of 70 medical personnel in a 22-hour operation to separate Siamese twins connected by a blood vessel in the back of their heads. Although each of the twins suffered some brain damage, both survived the surgery. Carson's operation marked the first time that twins joined at the head were successfully separated. The procedure owed its success in part to a technique developed by Carson: cooling the patients' bodies to the point where their blood stopped flowing. This kept the twins from bleeding to death while the surgeons separated their blood vessels.

Combines medicine with motivational speaking

Carson performs some 500 operations a year, nearly three times as many as a typical neurosurgeon. He also frequently speaks to children about how he overcame economic and social problems, motivating them to do the same. Carson has written more than 90 journal articles on neurosurgery and several books, including the best-sellers *Gifted Hands* (his 1990 autobiography) and *Think Big: Unleashing Your Potential for Excellence* (1992).

Carson has earned twenty-four honorary degrees, dozens of national citations of merit, and several awards, including *Ebony* magazine's American Black Achievement Award (1988), the Paul Harris Fellow from Rotary International (1988), and the Candle Award from Morehouse College (1989). In 1994 Carson and his wife set up the Carson Scholars Fund, which provides scholarships to deserving and financially needy students.

◻ SIGMUND FREUD (1856–1939)

Austrian neurologist and psychiatrist

Sigmund Freud was one of the world's foremost authorities on the workings of the human mind. He discovered that some illnesses originate in the mind, not the body. Freud identified sexuality and aggression as the two strongest factors shaping human behavior and dreams as the best clue to understanding how these forces work. He also explored how instinct-driven and conscience-driven behaviors clash and how the conflict between the two is resolved. Many terms invented by Freud—such as Oedipus complex, sibling rivalry, libido, ego, and id—are now part of everyday vocabulary.

Intellectual talent realized at young age

Sigismund Solomon Freud (he shortened his first name to "Sigmund" as a teenager) was born on May 6, 1856, in Freiburg, then part of the Austrian Empire and now the town of Pribor, in the Czech Republic. He was the first child born to his father's new wife, who later had seven more children. His father also had two sons from his first wife. Freud's father was a German Jew who had left his native land to escape anti-Jewish persecution.

The family moved to Vienna, the German-speaking capital of the Austrian Empire, when Freud was four years old. Freud would remain there for most of the rest of his life. His parents recognized his extraordinary intelligence at an early age, and they did not try to hide the fact that he was their favorite child. As a result, Freud developed a lifelong confidence in his abilities.

Sigmund Freud. (Reproduced by permission of the Corbis Corporation.)

Education and early work in medicine

Freud was an excellent student who usually ranked at the top of his class. In 1873, at the age of seventeen, he enrolled at the University of Vienna to study medicine. Freud found that he had an interest in several subjects, such as zoology (the study of animal life) and physiology (the study of the functions of living things), and thus took eight years to complete what was normally a five-year university program.

Freud researched physiology for one year after his 1881 graduation and then practiced medicine at the General Hospital in Vienna from 1882

to 1885. There he worked in several departments, including surgery, skin diseases, internal medicine, nervous diseases, and psychiatry (the study of the mind and the diagnosis, treatment, and prevention of emotional and behavioral disorders). He found that his greatest interest lay in psychiatry.

Develops "talking cure"

While Freud was on staff at the hospital, a colleague named Josef Breuer told him about a patient named Bertha Pappenheim who had become sick while caring for her terminally ill father. Breuer could find no physical cause for Pappenheim's symptoms: headaches, loss of appetite, coughing, weakness, and more. Breuer had found that when she discussed painful memories and the feelings they created in her, some of her symptoms decreased. Breuer theorized that some of Pappenheim's symptoms had begun when she had held back, or "repressed," her reaction to a difficult situation. With further discussion, Pappenheim's symptoms finally disappeared. She credited her recovery to this "talking cure."

Forms basis of psychoanalysis

In 1886 Freud married a woman named Martha Bernays; they eventually had six children. As his family grew, Freud moved his medical practice to his home so he could spend more time with his children.

When patients presented symptoms for which Freud could find no physical cause, he would explore the possibility of a mind-based disorder. Freud soon realized the importance of the sexual drive—or the "libido," as he called it—to mental and physical health. At that time, society considered the discussion of sexual matters unacceptable. Freud, however, argued that the stress of always repressing sexual memories, thoughts, and impulses created a host of physical problems.

Freud sought to support his theory by becoming his own test subject. He underwent "self-analysis" by examining his memories and thoughts, and concluded that many of his childhood memories were sexual, aggressive, or violent in nature. He recalled that he had been attracted to his mother, had viewed his father as a competitor for his mother's attention, and had felt an extreme jealousy toward his younger brother. From these self-discoveries Freud concluded that every child had similar memories. His self-analysis formed the basis of psychoanalysis, a method of treating emotional disorders that involves sessions during which the patient is encouraged to talk freely about personal experiences, especially about early childhood memories and dreams.

Freud came to believe that sexuality and aggression were the two main forces that shaped human behavior. He invented the term "Oedipus complex" to describe a boy's attraction to his mother and "Electra complex" for a girl's attraction to her father; the two names were taken from characters in an ancient Greek tragedy. He called the jealousy and competitiveness between siblings "sibling rivalry."

Dream analysis and the structure of the mind

Another area of psychiatry for which Freud is well known is dream analysis. In his 1899 book *The Interpretation of Dreams* he explained that dreams provide the best clues to how aggression and sexuality work in the mind. Over time Freud's works came to the attention of a wider group of physicians, and by 1910 he had achieved worldwide fame.

One of Freud's most influential later books, *The Ego and the Id* (1923), presented a framework for understanding the structure of the human mind. Freud separated the mind into three sections: the *id,* which is driven by instinct, the *superego,* which is driven by a person's conscience, and the *ego,* which works to integrate the id and the superego. Freud explained that when these three portions of the mind have conflicts that are left unresolved, a mental illness can result.

In 1923, Freud, a heavy cigar-smoker, had the first of several operations for cancer of the jaw. He died of his illness on September 23, 1939.

◻ ROBERT GALLO (1937–)

American AIDS researcher

Robert Charles Gallo is best known as one of the discoverers of the human immunodeficiency virus (HIV), the virus that causes acquired immunodeficiency syndrome (AIDS; see essay The AIDS Pandemic in this chapter). Gallo proved the cause-and-effect relationship between HIV and AIDS. He also developed a blood test to identify the presence of HIV.

In the mid-1980s, Gallo's role in discovering HIV was cast into doubt. French scientist Luc Montagnier (1932–) charged that Gallo had merely renamed and claimed as his own a virus sample that Montagnier had sent him. Although an investigative committee of the National Institutes of Health (NIH) found Gallo guilty of scientific misconduct in 1992, he appealed and was cleared of wrongdoing the following year. Today Gallo remains one of the world's most influential AIDS researchers.

Sister's death influences career path

Gallo was born on March 23, 1937, in Waterbury, Connecticut, and grew up in the home his Italian immigrant grandparents had bought. Gallo's father was the owner of a welding company who spent long hours at his job.

The defining event of Gallo's childhood, and a tragedy that tore his family apart, was the death of his only sibling—his sister Judith—from childhood leukemia (a type of cancer that affects the blood, bone marrow, and spleen). After Judith's death, Gallo grew close to Marcus Cox, the pathologist (a scientist who studies the cause and nature of diseases) who diagnosed her condition. Gallo became very interested in medical research and even occasionally accompanied Cox to the hospital.

Gallo chose to major in biology in college, graduating from Providence College in Rhode Island with a bachelor's degree (with high honors) in 1959. He then attended Jefferson Medical College in Philadelphia, earning his medical degree in 1963. In 1961 Gallo married a woman from his hometown named Mary Jane Hayes; they eventually had two children.

Conducts cancer research

Gallo conducted his medical residency at the University of Chicago, an institution known for its research on the biology of blood cells (Gallo's main interest). During his two years there, Gallo researched the biosynthesis (the creation of a compound by the body) of hemoglobin, the protein found in red blood cells that carries oxygen.

In 1965 Gallo accepted a research position at the NIH in Bethesda, Maryland, where he studied the causes of leukemia and the effectiveness of drug treatments for cancer patients. In 1971 Gallo was named head of the newly created Laboratory of Tumor Cell Biology at the National Cancer Institute (NCI; part of the NIH). In that capacity he discovered the first human leukemia virus—the agent that causes leukemia—as well as a number of oncogenes (cancer-causing material that is carried in genes).

Robert Gallo.
(Reproduced by
permission of Archive
Photos, Inc.)

Determines cause of AIDS

In 1981, doctors in the United States first diagnosed AIDS, a fatal disease in which the immune system becomes severely weakened, leaving the patient unable to fight off a wide range of illnesses. Gallo's interest and expertise in viruses led him to try to identify the cause of AIDS. In 1982, the NCI formed an AIDS task force and named Gallo as the chair. On April 3, 1984, Gallo announced that he had found the probable cause of AIDS—

HIV—and that he had developed a blood test that could detect the presence of HIV.

For the next ten years, Gallo endured a storm of controversy as to whether he had used Luc Montagnier's work at the Pasteur Institute in Paris in identifying HIV without crediting Montagnier. In 1990, during the height of the controversy, Gallo told his side of the story in his book *Virus Hunting—AIDS, Cancer, and the Human Retrovirus: A Story of Scientific Discovery*. In 1993 Gallo was cleared of any wrongdoing in the affair. Gallo and Montagnier are now considered co-discoverers of the virus, while Gallo retains credit for having developed the blood test.

Founds Institute of Human Virology

In 1995 Gallo became director of the newly built, multimillion-dollar Institute of Human Virology (IHV) at the University of Maryland in Baltimore. There Gallo worked to develop AIDS treatments and an AIDS vaccine. In 2001 Gallo made headlines with his announcement that he was prepared to begin testing an AIDS vaccine on human subjects. His experimental vaccine, which produces antibodies that worked on a variety of HIV strains from around the world, showed promising results in trials on monkeys.

JOHN HEYSHAM GIBBON JR. (1903–1973)

American surgeon

John H. Gibbon Jr. is best known as the inventor of the heart-lung machine, a pump that circulates blood around the heart and enriches it with oxygen. The heart-lung machine takes over a patient's cardiac and respiratory (breathing) functions while the patient is undergoing heart or lung surgery. Gibbon first used his machine successfully during an open-heart operation in 1953, beginning the modern era of open-heart surgery.

A fifth-generation physician

Gibbon was born in Philadelphia on September 29, 1903, to John Heysham Gibbon and Marjorie Young Gibbon. He was the second of four children. The elder John Gibbon was a surgeon, as had been three generations of Gibbon men before him. The younger John Gibbon attended Princeton University for his undergraduate education, earning a bachelor of arts degree in 1923. Four years later he completed his medical degree at Jefferson Medical College in Philadelphia. He then worked as an intern at Pennsylvania Hospital from 1927 to 1929.

Gibbon began his medical career in 1930 as a research fellow in surgery at Harvard Medical School. The next year he married Mary Hopkinson, a surgical researcher, and took a position at the University of Pennsylvania School of Medicine as a fellow in medicine. In 1934 he returned to Harvard to accept a second surgical fellowship.

Develops heart-lung machine

Gibbon had first become interested in a machine that could oxygenate blood in 1931, when he witnessed the death of a woman who had a blood clot on her lung. Because of the clot, blood could not pass through the lungs to receive necessary oxygen. Gibbon believed that if doctors had had a device that could oxygenate blood, they could have performed surgery on the woman's lungs and removed the clot. Taking that idea one step further, he thought that if the machine could also pump blood around the heart, it could be used during heart surgery as well.

When Gibbon returned to Harvard, he began working in earnest to develop a heart-lung machine. His earliest model, which he successfully used during an experimental operation on a cat on May 10, 1935, used tubes to remove blood from a vein, supply the blood with oxygen, and route it back into an artery. Gibbon kept the cat alive by this artificial means for fifty minutes; the cat's heart function then returned to normal and continued working for several hours. By 1939, after several more experiments, Gibbon had greatly extended the survival period for animal subjects.

John Gibbon.
(Reproduced by permission of the Corbis Corporation.)

Becomes professor of surgery

In 1937 Gibbon began working as a surgeon at Pennsylvania Hospital. Three years later, during World War II (1939–45), he joined the U.S. Army Reserves medical corps. From 1942 to 1944 Gibbon was on active duty in the South Pacific and was promoted to the rank of lieutenant colonel. He then spent a year as chief of surgical service at Mayo General Hospital in Galensburg, Illinois.

Gibbon returned to Jefferson Medical College in 1946 to serve as professor of surgery, director of surgical research, and attending surgeon at the college's hospital. He remained at Jefferson for ten years, during which time he also served as chair of the editorial board for the professional journal *Annals of Surgery.*

Uses heart-lung machine on a human

Throughout his years at Jefferson, Gibbon continued to improve the design of his heart-lung machine and to test the machine on cats and dogs. His device came to the attention of the company IBM, which built three experimental machines: the model I heart-lung machine in 1949, the model II oxygenator in 1951, and the model III oxygenator in 1954.

On May 6, 1953, Gibbon used a heart-lung machine while performing surgery on a human patient for the first time. He successfully repaired a heart defect in an eighteen-year-old girl named Cecelia Bavolek. The patient was connected to the machine for forty-five minutes; for twenty-six of those minutes the machine entirely took over her cardiac and respiratory functions.

Gibbon continued performing surgery and teaching at a number of institutions—including Jefferson Medical Center, Pennsylvania Hospital, the Veterans Administration Hospital in Philadelphia, Baylor Medical College, and Harvard Medical School—until his retirement in 1967. He also served as a member, fellow, or officer of several professional organizations, such as the American College of Surgeons and the Pennsylvania Medical Society. He received numerous awards from medical societies in the United States and abroad. Gibbon died of a massive heart attack while playing tennis on February 5, 1973.

ALICE HAMILTON (1869–1970)

Pathologist and founder of occupational medicine

Alice Hamilton was the first medical doctor to investigate ailments suffered by workers in industrial settings. Her discoveries played an important role in the passage of laws concerning workplace safety and worker compensation. Hamilton's 1925 book *Industrial Poisons* laid the foundation for the new field of industrial medicine. She also made medical history by becoming the first female faculty member at Harvard Medical School.

Explores health problems in factories

Hamilton was born into a wealthy family on February 27, 1869, in New York City. When Hamilton was just six weeks old, her family moved to Fort Wayne, Indiana. She and her three sisters were educated at home and in private schools; their mother encouraged them to expand their intellect and to assert their independence.

Interested in medicine from an early age, Hamilton attended the Fort Wayne College of Medicine for two years. She then transferred to the Uni-

Medicine

BIOGRAPHIES

versity of Michigan, completing her medical degree in 1893. In 1897, following internships at universities in Minneapolis, Boston, and Germany, Hamilton was hired as a professor of pathology (the field of medicine that studies the causes and nature of diseases) at the Woman's Medical School at Northwestern University in Evanston, Illinois (near Chicago). Five years later she also assumed the post of bacteriologist (a scientist who studies bacteria) at the Memorial Institute for Infectious Diseases in Chicago.

Fights for public health and occupational health measures

Shortly after arriving in Chicago, Hamilton moved into Hull House, a settlement house (an organization devoted to the improvement of neighborhood life) that served immigrant factory workers. It was established by social welfare activist Jane Addams (1860–1935) in 1889 to provide a range of social and economic services to poor people. During her time at Hull House, Hamilton started medical education classes and a well-baby clinic. From her work with Hull House's clients, Hamilton learned about the range of health problems factory workers faced due to dangerous conditions (particularly the use of toxic materials). She was also shocked by the poverty and disease she witnessed in the working-class neighborhood.

In 1902 a typhoid fever epidemic struck Chicago. (Typhoid fever is a highly infectious disease characterized by a high fever and severe digestive problems.) Hamilton pointed out that flies, attracted to untreated sewage, spread disease, and she urged the local health department

Alice Hamilton. (Reproduced by permission of AP/Wide World Photos.)

to improve sanitation conditions. At the same time, Hamilton made public her conclusion that unsafe machinery and toxic chemicals, particularly lead dust, were harming the people who worked in factories. Since there were no worker protection laws, when a worker got sick from the unhealthy conditions, his employer could simply fire him and hire a new worker who needed employment.

Heads state commission on industrial poisons

In 1910, Hamilton persuaded the governor of Illinois to establish a state commission to study industrial poisons with her as the head; it was the first such commission in the world. As a result of the commission's findings, the Illinois state government passed a series of worker compensation laws, laws that require compensation for workers who become sickened or hurt on the job.

Hamilton worked for the U.S. Department of Labor from 1911 to 1921, investigating the dangers of lead and phosphorus use in industry. She found that many companies—particularly those in mining and in the production of rubber, paint, gasoline, and steel—provided inadequate, if any, protection for workers using toxic materials. She also discovered that the use of lead in facilities with poor ventilation endangered workers' health. Hamilton was able to persuade many plant owners to make changes to protect their workers even before federal laws governing workplace safety were passed in the 1920s and 1930s.

Hamilton was also heavily involved in the peace movement during the 1910s and 1920s. She traveled to Europe to urge an end to World War I (1914–18) and helped found the Women's International League for Peace and Freedom.

Joins Harvard faculty

In 1919 Hamilton accepted the position of professor of industrial medicine at Harvard University Medical School, becoming the first woman on the faculty. Because Hamilton was female, the school made her agree not to use the Faculty Club, not to receive football tickets, and not to march in graduation ceremonies. All of Hamilton's students were male, as Harvard Medical School did not admit female students until the mid-1940s.

In the 1920s and 1930s, Hamilton continued to study workplace safety and industrial health. She expanded her investigations to include working conditions abroad, and in 1924 she served as the only female delegate to the League of Nations Health Commission. (The League of Nations was the forerunner of the United Nations; it was established as a world peace-making body in 1919.) In 1934 Hamilton published the classic book *Industrial Toxicology.*

Hamilton retired from Harvard in 1935, after which she worked as a consultant to the U.S. Department of Labor. She wrote her autobiography, *Exploring the Dangerous Trades,* in 1943 and from 1944 to 1949 served as president of the National Consumers League, a nonprofit group that fought for consumer safety in the marketplace and in the workplace. Hamilton continued investigating the use of toxic substances in factories until she was in her late eighties. She devoted her final years to gardening and painting and in 1970 died at the age of 100 in Hadlyme, Connecticut.

◻ JOHN ROCK (1890–1984)
American gynecologist and obstetrician

John Rock was a leading expert on the female reproductive system and a key player in the quest to develop the birth-control pill. Rock's original intention in studying the female hormone progesterone was to help women who were having trouble conceiving to become pregnant. Rock later teamed up with other researchers in developing a type of progesterone that could be taken in pill form to prevent pregnancy. Rock conducted the tests necessary for the pill to be approved by the U.S. Food and Drug Administration (FDA). A devout Roman Catholic, Rock then challenged the Church hierarchy's opposition to birth control (see essay Issues and Developments in Birth Control in this chapter) and made moral arguments for usage of "the pill."

A roundabout path to medicine

Rock was born on March 24, 1890, in Marlborough, Massachusetts. He was one of five children of businessman Frank Sylvester Rock and Ann Jane (Murphy) Rock. John Rock intended to follow in his father's footsteps and go into a career in business. He graduated from Boston High School of Commerce and worked as an accountant for two firms, both of which fired him. Rock then decided to attend college.

He enrolled at Harvard University, graduating with a bachelor's degree in 1915 and a medical degree in 1918. Rock performed his internship at Massachusetts General Hospital and remained there for his residency in urology (the study of the urinary tract). He next spent a year as a surgeon at the Brookline Free Hospital for Women, after which he opened a private practice. In 1922 Rock also began serving as an assistant professor of obstetrics (the study of childbirth and the health of women during childbirth) at Harvard Medical School.

Opens fertility clinic

In the mid-1920s Rock opened a fertility clinic at the Free Hospital for Women to address women's reproductive problems. There he teamed up with Harvard scientist Miriam F. Menkin in an effort to fertilize a human egg in a test tube. The pair's research was later used by **Patrick Steptoe** (1913–1988; see biography in this chapter) and others to develop human embryos in the laboratory that could be implanted in the mother's uterus. (The first "test-tube baby," Louise Brown, was born in 1978.)

By the 1950s, Rock had turned his attention to another method he hoped would aid fertility: the use of the female hormone progesterone. During pregnancy, a woman's body produces progesterone to prevent the ovaries from releasing any eggs; as a result, while the woman is pregnant she cannot conceive. Rock believed that a if woman who was having problems conceiving took progesterone, it would allow her reproductive system to "rest." Then, when she went off the progesterone, her fertility would increase.

Explores contraceptive properties of progesterone

In the mid-1950s, the purpose of Rock's research shifted from encouraging pregnancies to preventing them. The cause for this change was Rock's contact with scientists Gregory Pincus (1903–1967) and Min Chueh Chang (1908–1991), both of whom were interested in developing a synthetic (manufactured in a laboratory) version of progesterone that could be taken orally to prevent pregnancy. Working together, the trio developed a contraceptive pill.

When Rock turned sixty-five years of age, he retired from his post at the Free Hospital and opened the Rock Reproductive Clinic. He then tested the contraceptive pill on groups of female volunteers in Puerto Rico, Haiti, and Mexico. (Rock believed that "the pill" would cause controversy in the United States and decided to run trials elsewhere.) Of all the women in the study who took the pill according to directions, none became pregnant. On May 9, 1960, the FDA approved the birth-control pill, and GD Searle & Company began marketing it under the name Enovid. By 1964 4 million Americans were taking the pill; that number had grown to 100 million worldwide by 1998.

Challenges the Roman Catholic Church

After the FDA had approved the oral contraceptive, Rock shifted his focus to public opinion. As a devout Roman Catholic, Rock was well-prepared to challenge the Church's opposition to all non-natural forms of birth control. (The only method of birth control approved by the Church was the "rhythm method," in which couples chose not to have sexual intercourse during those times of the month when the woman was most likely to conceive.) He made his case for using the pill in family planning and population control in his 1963 book *The Time Has Come: A Catholic Doctor's Proposals to End the Battle Over Birth Control.* Pope Paul IV (1897–1978), in response to Rock's arguments, appointed a papal commission to study the issue. Although the commission recommended that the Church drop its opposition to the pill, Church leaders set aside the commission's findings and continued to oppose artificial birth control. Despite the ruling, Rock remained a committed Roman Catholic and attended mass daily until his death on December 4, 1984, at age ninety-four.

◻ FLORENCE SABIN (1871–1953)

American physician

Florence Sabin was one of the leading female scientists of her time and an influential promoter of equal rights for women. She was the first female full professor at Johns Hopkins School of Medicine and the first woman elected president of the American Association of Anatomists. Sabin was best known for her findings on the origin of the lymphatic system and the response of the immune system to infection. She advanced scientific understanding of the workings and treatment of tuberculosis (an extremely contagious lung disease) and helped transform anatomy from a field that merely described parts of the body to one that focused on the connections between form and function. After her retirement, Sabin pressed for stronger regulations to protect public health.

Florence Sabin. (Reproduced by permission of FPG International LLC.)

Blazes trail for women in education

Sabin was born in Central City, Colorado, on November 9, 1871. Her father was a mining engineer, and her mother was a teacher. At the age of four, Sabin moved with her family to Denver. After her mother died three years later, Sabin, her sisters, and her father went to live with Sabin's uncle in Lake Forest, Illinois. Sabin attended boarding school in Vermont and then went to the all-women's Smith College in Massachusetts.

Sabin discovered her passion for science and math in college and earned a bachelor of science degree in 1893. Three years later she enrolled in the Johns Hopkins Medical School in Baltimore—one of the few medical institutions that admitted women at the time—and chose to concentrate on anatomy (the study of the structure and form of biological organisms). After graduating with a medical degree in 1900, Sabin realized she was more interested in teaching and research than in practicing medicine. She took a position in the department of anatomy at Johns Hopkins. In 1901 she published a well-received textbook on anatomy titled *An Atlas of the Medulla and Midbrain.*

Discovers origins of lymphatic system

Sabin launched her career by studying the lymphatic system (the network of lymph glands or nodes that carries infection-fighting white blood cells throughout the body). She wanted to solve the question of whether lymphatic vessels form independently of, or arise from, blood vessels—something that doctors had been trying to figure out for some time. To that end, Sabin studied pig embryos in very early stages of development. She discovered that lymphatics sprouted from veins and grew outward, eventually connecting with one another, and wrote an award-winning book detailing her findings: *The Origin and Development of the Lymphatic System* (1903).

In 1905 Sabin was appointed associate professor of anatomy at Johns Hopkins, and in 1917 she became the university's first female full professor. She continued to study the development of blood cells—in particular white blood cells (called monocytes) that attack infectious bacteria—in embryos. Sabin's work drew the interest of the National Tuberculosis Association, which presented her with a research grant. At the time, tuberculosis was a major health problem nationwide, and understanding how the body responded to invasion by tuberculosis-causing bacteria was a necessary first step toward finding a cure.

Promotes women's rights, public health

Throughout her career, Sabin argued for the rights of women to equal opportunities in education, employment, and scientific research. She also campaigned for the right of women to vote, which was achieved in 1920 with the passage of the Nineteenth Amendment to the Constitution. Although Sabin had overcome many of the barriers that women scientists faced, she could not overcome all of them. In 1925, when the position of head of the department of anatomy at Johns Hopkins became available, Sabin applied. She was passed over for the position, however, in favor of one of her former students. That same year she became the first woman elected as a member of the National Academy of Sciences.

Sabin then left Johns Hopkins for a position with the Rockefeller Institute for Medical Research (now Rockefeller University) in New York City. There she continued her study of how white blood cells fight tuberculosis and other infections. She also began a new study on the formation of antibodies (proteins produced by certain cells of the body in response to invasion by specific disease-causing foreign substances).

Sabin retired in 1938 and moved back to Denver to take a post with the Denver public health-care system. She spent her remaining years pushing for improved public health regulations and the construction of additional health-care facilities. The Sabin Health Laws, which Sabin helped pass, called for strict regulations controlling infectious disease, milk pasteurization (the process of heating milk to kill bacteria), and sewage disposal.

Sabin died of a heart attack on October 3, 1953. In her honor, the state of Colorado erected a bronze statue bearing her likeness in the National Statuary Hall in Washington, D.C. (Each state is permitted to place two statues in the hall, in remembrance of its most respected citizens. Colorado's other statue is of astronaut Jack Swigert.)

◻ THOMAS E. STARZL (1926–)
American surgeon and researcher

Thomas E. Starzl conducted groundbreaking research in organ transplantation (see essay The Development of Organ Transplantation in this chapter) and was the first person to successfully transplant a human liver. Some of his most important work dealt with developing a way to keep the body from rejecting transplanted organs. In 1985 Starzl established a transplantation institute at the University of Pittsburgh Medical Center that now bears his name. After his retirement in 1991, Starzl researched xenotransplantation, which is the process of transplanting animal organs into humans.

Makes career choice at early age
Starzl was born on March 11, 1926, in LeMars, Iowa, into a strict German Catholic family. His father was the publisher of the small town's newspaper, and his mother was a surgical nurse. Starzl's mother was a great influence on her son's career choice; by age eleven Starzl knew he wanted to be a surgeon.

Starzl was an outstanding student in high school. In addition to his studies, he worked on his father's paper, played football and basketball, was on the debate team, and played trumpet in the band. After graduation Starzl attended Westminster College in Fulton, Missouri, and then went to Northwestern University Medical School in Chicago. At the same time, he went through the school's doctoral program in neurophysiology, and by 1952 he had earned both his Ph.D. and his M.D. (with distinction).

Starzl then performed a series of surgical residencies at Johns Hopkins University, the University of Miami, and the Veterans Administration Hospital in Chicago. In 1958 he returned to Northwestern to work as a surgeon and conduct research in the newly developing field of liver transplantation.

Works on liver transplantation
In 1962 Starzl, who by then was married and had three children, joined the faculty of the University of Colorado School of Medicine in Denver. There he spent long hours experimenting with liver transplants in ani-

mals. He found that the most challenging aspect of transplantation was overcoming the immune system's attempt to destroy the new organ.

After a year's research, Starzl was ready to try a liver transplant on a human subject. The first attempt was unsuccessful; the patient bled to death during the operation. Starzl was harshly criticized and advised to give up his quest. However, he continued his research and by 1967 was ready to try again. That year he successfully transplanted a liver into a young girl; she lived for thirteen months after the operation. Encouraged by the results, Starzl went ahead with many more transplants—a total of more than 200 liver transplants and 1,000 kidney transplants between the years 1967 and 1980.

Starzl's success with transplantation was largely due to his development and usage of azathioprine, corticosteroid, and cyclosporine, drugs that prevented the immune system from rejecting the organs. His developments helped advance the field of organ transplantation from the experimental stage to an accepted mainstream treatment for patients with end-stage kidney or liver disease.

Advances transplant practices in Pittsburgh

In 1981 Starzl became a professor of surgery at the University of Pittsburgh School of Medicine. He also worked as chief of transplantation services for the city's Presbyterian University Hospital, Children's Hospital, and the Veterans Affairs Medical Center. Ten years later Starzl was hired as director of the University of Pittsburgh Transplantation Institute, which in 1996 was renamed the Thomas E. Starzl Transplantation Institute.

Thomas Starzl. (Reproduced by permission of the Corbis Corporation.)

In 1991, when Starzl was sixty-five, he stopped performing surgery but continued to conduct research and teach at the University of Pittsburgh. Throughout the 1990s he focused much of his energy on the emerging field of xenotransplantation. (The shortage of human organs available for transplantation has made using animal organs an attractive option.) Starzl's surgical team made medical history in 1992 and 1993 when they transplanted two baboon livers into human recipients.

Starzl is one of the most-published scientists today, with more than 2,000 scientific papers, as well as four books and 283 chapters in books, to his name. He is also an active member of international transplant organizations that help shape policies concerning how organ recipients are selected from the long waiting lists.

☐ PATRICK STEPTOE (1913–1988)
British gynecologist and medical researcher

Patrick Steptoe, together with British physiologist (a scientist who studies the functions of living organisms) Robert G. Edwards (1925–), pioneered *in vitro* (in an artificial environment) fertilization (IVF), a technique that made possible the birth of the first "test-tube baby" in 1978. IVF, designed to help women who are having problems becoming pregnant, involves removing eggs from a woman's ovary and fertilizing them with sperm in the lab. The developing embryo is then transferred to the mother's uterus, where pregnancy progresses normally. While IVF is considered a medical triumph, it has sparked intense ethical debates.

Education and military service
Steptoe was born on June 9, 1913, in rural Oxfordshire, England, to a father who was a church organist and a mother who was a social worker. Steptoe studied medicine at St. George Hospital Medical School in London, earning his medical degree in 1939. Later that year, at the start of World War II (1939–45), he volunteered as a surgeon with the Royal Navy. During a sea battle against the Italian forces in 1941, Steptoe's ship sank and the Italians took him and other British sailors prisoner. At first Steptoe enjoyed special privileges because he was a surgeon. After he was caught assisting other prisoners to escape, however, his captors placed him in solitary confinement. Steptoe won his freedom in 1943 as part of a prisoner exchange agreement.

Continues medical career
After he completed his military service in 1946, Steptoe began advanced studies in obstetrics and gynecology (fields concerned with childbirth and the health of the female reproductive system). In 1948 he was named a member of the Royal College of Obstetricians and Gynecologists. He then moved to Manchester and opened a private practice. Three years later he moved to Oldham, in northeast England, to become senior obstetrician and gynecologist at the Oldham General and District Hospital.

In the early 1950s Steptoe became concerned about the problem of infertility in women, which was then commonly treated with surgery. In his search for a safer and more effective means of aiding fertility, Steptoe devised a tool, called a laproscope, to better examine and understand the reproductive system. A laproscope is a thin, flexible tube tipped with a fiberoptic light. When inserted into the abdomen, it allows a doctor to see blocked Fallopian tubes (a major cause of infertility) and to perform minimally invasive surgery to correct the problem.

Devises test-tube baby procedure

In 1968 Steptoe teamed up with Robert Edwards of Cambridge University to continue seeking alternative methods of treating infertility. While Steptoe had invented a method of retrieving eggs from women with blocked Fallopian tubes, Edwards had figured out how to fertilize eggs with sperm in the laboratory. The pair worked to perfect their procedures and to get the zygote (fertilized egg) to develop properly.

Steptoe and Edwards first attempted to implant a fertilized egg into a woman's uterus in 1972; however, the egg failed to develop into an embryo. Despite a storm of criticism from the public and the media over their unusual methods, Steptoe and Edwards continued their research. They finally succeeded in 1977, when they implanted the zygote into a young woman who was unable to conceive due to blocked Fallopian tubes. The embryo developed normally, and the baby, named Louise Joy Brown, was born on July 25, 1978. The media compared the birth of the world's first "test-tube baby" to the first moon landing in importance.

Patrick Steptoe. (Reproduced by permission of AP/Wide World Photos.)

Procedure sparks debate

In response to the news of baby Louise's birth, many women with trouble conceiving sought Steptoe's help. At the same time, the Roman Catholic Church and other religious groups began to oppose IVF as morally objectionable and accused Steptoe and Edwards of "playing God." Over time, however, the demand for IVF services increased, and the controversy faded. One aspect of the debate that still continues today regards the ethics of storing frozen embryos over extended periods of time for future implantation—namely, are these stored embryos property or people?

There are presently more than 300 clinics in the United States that provide aid to infertile couples; IVF is the most popular service offered.

Some 500,000 babies worldwide were conceived through IVF between the years 1978 and 2000.

In 1980, Steptoe and Edwards founded the Bourn Hall Clinic near Cambridge, England, as a research and treatment center for infertility. The pair co-authored their scientific memoirs in 1981: *A Matter of Life*. Steptoe continued to pursue his work until his death from cancer in 1988.

BRIEF BIOGRAPHIES ◣

◤ VIRGINIA APGAR (1909–1974)

American anesthesiologist (a medical doctor who administers numbing medication to patients) and public health practitioner who developed a method for evaluating newborn babies that is now widely used around the world. The Apgar Score System measures a newborn's condition in five categories (color, heart rate, muscle tone, breathing effort, and response to stimulation) and assigns a score of 0, 1, or 2 for each category, with 2 being the best. Apgar also studied the effects on babies of anesthetics given to mothers during delivery. She spent the last fifteen years of her life working for the March of Dimes, a nonprofit organization that works to reduce infant mortality.

◤ SIR FREDERICK GRANT BANTING (1891–1941)

Canadian physician and physiologist (a scientist who studies the functions and actions of life or living matter) who, along with physiologist Charles H. Best (1899–1978), discovered insulin, a hormone secreted by the pancreas that regulates sugar in the blood. Insulin is now widely used as a treatment for controlling diabetes, a fatal disease characterized by the body's inability to process sugars due to the inadequate production or use of insulin; this results in an elevated blood sugar level. In 1923 Banting became the first Canadian to win the Nobel Prize in physiology or medicine for his discovery; angry that Best was not awarded the prize along with him, Banting split the award money with his colleague. He was killed in a plane crash while on a war mission in World War II (1939–45).

◤ ALFRED BINET (1857–1911)

French psychologist known for his significant contributions to the field of child psychology. Binet, together with his colleague Theodore Simon, developed the Binet-Simon intelligence quotient (IQ) test. As director of an experimental psychology clinic at the Sorbonne in Paris, Binet wanted to come up with a method to measure the mental age of a child (the degree to which the child is advanced mentally), in order to identify slow learners so they can be helped. The test he developed with Simon evaluated a child's ability to follow commands, copy patterns, sort objects, and complete other tasks. By dividing the child's mental age by his or her chronological age, the tester could figure the child's intelligence quotient, or IQ. Although intelligence tests such as the Binet-Simon test remain popular, they have become controversial in recent years due to the belief that they do not accurately measure a person's true intelligence.

◢ ALEXA CANADY (1950–)

One of the foremost children's neurosurgeons (a doctor who performs surgery on nerve tissue) in the country and the first African American woman noted for excellence in neurosurgery. Canady is an expert in the treatment of brain injuries and has developed new methods of treating life-threatening conditions such as gunshot wounds. She has written extensively on pediatric neurosurgery. Canady has received honors and awards from more than twenty organizations, including the Athena Award from the University of Michigan Alumni Association in 1995. In 1993 she became chief of neurosurgery at the Children's Hospital in Detroit and a professor at Wayne State University School of Medicine.

◢ BORIS ERNST CHAIN (1906–1979)

Alfred Binet.
(Reproduced by permission of the Archives of the History of American Psychology.)

German-born British biochemist (a scientist who studies the chemistry of living matter) who, with Australian-English pathologist (a scientist who studies diseases) Howard Florey (1898–1968), isolated and purified penicillin. Scottish scientist Alexander Fleming (1881–1955; see box on page 214) had discovered the antibacterial properties of the *penicillium* mold in the late 1920s. In 1938 Chain and Florey teamed up to study the effects of penicillin and to purify, test, and develop the drug for human use. Widespread penicillin production began in 1942, and the drug was widely used to treat soldiers during World War II (1939–45; see essay The Discovery, Importance, and Limitations of Antibiotics in this chapter). In 1945 Chain shared the Nobel Prize in physiology or medicine with Fleming and Florey for their development of penicillin.

◿ SIR JOHN CHARNLEY (1911–1982)

British surgeon and creator of the techniques and materials necessary for total hip replacement (THR) surgery. THR is now a common procedure; by replacing a worn-out hip joint with an artificial one, it restores mobility and a high quality of life to patients who previously experienced chronic, severe pain. Charnley served as an orthopedic surgeon (a doctor concerned with disorders of the skeletal system) with the Royal Army Medical Corps during World War II (1939–45) and developed many orthopedic devices and instruments to help disabled soldiers. In the 1960s he developed his method of attaching an artificial hip joint to the inside of the femur (thigh bone).

◿ HARVEY WILLIAMS CUSHING (1869–1939)

American neurosurgeon (a doctor who performs surgery on nerve tissue) who was considered the greatest brain surgeon of his time. Cushing invented many basic neurosurgical procedures, advanced understanding of brain injuries and diseases, and developed methods of operating on tumors (growths) that were previously considered inoperable. Cushing was also an expert on medical history; he served as director of history of medicine studies at Yale University from 1937 until his death.

Charles Drew.
(Reproduced by permission of AP/Wide World Photos.)

◿ CHARLES R. DREW (1904–1950)

African American physician and surgeon who established "blood banks" to preserve blood used for transfusions. Drew found that if he separated the blood cells from the plasma (the liquid portion of blood), it could be stored for longer periods of time. During World War II (1939–45) he helped set up blood banks in the United States and Great Britain. At the same time he fought policies of segregating (keeping separate) blood contributed by African Americans from the general supply. In the 1960s, the Charles R. Drew University of Medicine and Science was founded in Los Angeles. Drew, who was killed in a car crash in 1950, was honored with a U.S. postage stamp bearing his likeness in 1981.

◭ PHILIP DRINKER (1894–1972)

American engineer and inventor of the "iron lung," a machine that forces air in and out of the lungs. This invention saved the lives of many people, especially those with polio (a disease, often affecting children, that leads to permanent partial paralysis and deformities), who could not breathe on their own because the disease had paralyzed their lungs. The iron lung was also used to save people suffering from respiratory failure from gas poisoning, acute alcoholism, and other ailments. The need for the machine was greatly reduced once Jonas Salk (1914–1995) developed a vaccine for polio in 1955 (see box on page 202). Drinker was also a pioneer in the field of industrial health, campaigned for the use of protective devices by those who worked with dust and toxic fumes, and established early air quality standards for the U.S. government.

◭ ROBERT G. EDWARDS (1925–)

British physiologist (a doctor who studies the functions and actions of life or living matter) who, together with British medical researcher **Patrick Steptoe** (1913–1988; see biography in this chapter), pioneered *in vitro* fertilization, the technique of fertilizing eggs with sperm in the laboratory. Edwards and Steptoe invented a way to keep a fertilized egg alive in the laboratory. When the embryo reached a certain stage of development, they transferred it back into the mother's uterus. That process paved the way for the birth of the first "test-tube baby" in 1978. In vitro fertilization has helped many women have children who had been unable to conceive by natural means.

◭ PAUL EHRLICH (1854–1915)

German bacteriologist (a scientist who studies bacteria) who invented chemotherapy, the use of powerful chemicals to fight disease in the human body. One of Ehrlich's greatest accomplishments was the development of the drug Salvarsan, which was the first effective treatment for syphilis (an infectious, sexually transmitted disease that if left untreated can cause blindness and insanity). Ehrlich shared the Nobel Prize in physiology or medicine in 1908 with Russian biologist Ilya Mechnikov (1845–1916) for the pair's work in immunology (the branch of medicine concerned with the body's ability to protect itself from disease). Specifically, they explained how cells produced large quantities of protein chains to absorb toxins and prevent new infections.

◭ WILLEM EINTHOVEN (1860–1927)

Dutch physiologist (a scientist who studies the functions and actions of life or living matter) and inventor of the string galvanometer, an instrument used to measure the flow of small electric currents. Einthoven's galvanometer produced a recording of electrical activity of the heart known as an electrocardiogram (EKG). The EKG remains an essential tool for diagnosing certain types of heart disease. Throughout his career, Einthoven continued to perfect the string galvanometer and instructed medical personnel on how to interpret the recorded heart activity. He won the 1924 Nobel Prize in physiology or medicine for his invention.

◢ GERTRUDE BELLE ELION (1918–1999)

American biochemist (a scientist who studies the chemistry of living matter) whose research led to the discovery of many drug treatments for diseases such as leukemia, malaria, herpes, gout, and AIDS (see essay The AIDS Pandemic in this chapter). Elion also developed drugs that have been used to prevent a patient's body from rejecting transplanted organs. Elion and her colleague George H. Hitchings (1905–1998) won the Nobel Prize in physiology or medicine in 1988 for their contributions to the field of drug treatments.

◢ DANIEL CARELTON GAJDUSEK (1923–)

American virologist (a scientist who studies viruses), pediatrician, and discoverer of "slow viruses," viruses that remain inactive in the body for long periods before any signs of illness appear. Examples of diseases brought on by "slow viruses" are mad-cow disease and its associated disease in humans, called Creutzfeldt-Jakob disease, which attacks the brain and causes death. Gajdusek, who spent the latter part of his career as chief of the Laboratory of Central Nervous System Studies (part of the National Institutes of Health), won the Nobel Prize in physiology or medicine in 1976 for his work on infectious diseases.

◢ JOSEPH LEONARD GOLDSTEIN (1940–)

American geneticist (a scientist who studies inheritance in living organisms) who first described the process by which the human body accumulates and metabolizes (breaks down to provide energy) cholesterol. Goldstein's explanation of the relationship between cholesterol, blood lipids (fats), and heart disease is considered one of the most important medical findings of the twentieth century. His research paved the way for the development of drugs and dietary guidelines that can lower blood cholesterol levels and reduce the risk of heart disease. Goldstein won the Nobel Prize in physiology or medicine in 1985 for his work on cholesterol.

◢ WILLIAM AUGUSTUS HINTON (1883–1959)

American bacteriologist (a scientist who studies bacteria) and pathologist (a scientist who studies diseases) who overcame racial barriers to become the first African American professor at Harvard Medical School and the foremost authority of his time on venereal disease, particularly syphilis (an infectious, sexually transmitted disease that if left untreated can cause blindness and insanity). Hinton developed the first reliable blood test that could detect the presence of syphilis. The "Hinton Test" was a great improvement over earlier tests, which gave a large number of false positives (results in which people test positive for a disease even though they do not actually have it). As a consequence Hinton greatly reduced the number of patients subjected to needless treatment for syphilis. In addition to teaching at Harvard for more than 30 years, Hinton headed a biological laboratory at the Massachusetts Department of Public Health.

◢ CHARLES BRENTON HUGGINS (1901–1997)

American surgeon and winner of the Nobel Prize in physiology or medicine in 1966 for his discovery of the connection between hormones and cancer of the breast and prostate (an organ at the base of the bladder in males). Huggins's research set the stage for the development of hormone therapy, the first treatment for cancer that did not involve the use of toxic or radioactive chemicals. Huggins, a professor at the University of Chicago Medical School for most of his career, also investigated whether the birth control pill (see essay Issues and Developments in Birth Control in this chapter) increased a woman's likelihood of developing breast cancer; he concluded that it did not.

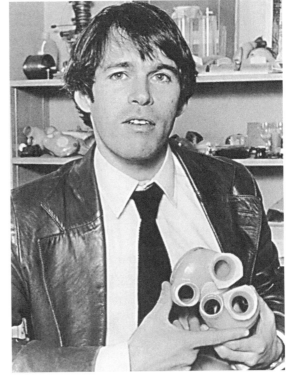

Robert Jarvik. (Reproduced by permission of the Corbis Corporation.)

◢ ROBERT KOFFLER JARVIK (1946–)

American physician, bioengineer (a scientist who applies engineering principles and techniques to problems in medicine and biology), and designer of the artificial heart (known as the Jarvik–7). The plastic, aluminum, and polyester organ was used in the mid-1980s to extend the lives of nearly fifty people—most of whom were on a waiting list for heart transplants. Because the Jarvik-7 achieved mixed results, and several people using it died from blood clots that formed on the artificial materials and lodged in their brains, the federal government outlawed its use on humans until further research could be done. In the late 1990s Jarvik was at work developing a new artificial heart, called the Jarvik 2000. The new model differs from the old in that it does not replace the natural heart but is inserted in the left ventricle and helps the heart pump blood.

◢ KARL LANDSTEINER (1868–1943)

Austrian-American immunologist (a scientist who studies the body's ability to protect itself from disease) and pathologist (a scientist who studies diseases) who researched the workings of the human immune system. Landsteiner discovered the existence of distinct blood types (A, B, and O; the rare type AB was identified later), which earned him the Nobel Prize in physiology or medicine in 1930. He determined that type O was a universal donor, meaning it could be used for transfusions with patients of all blood types. Landsteiner also isolated the virus that causes polio (a disease, often affecting children, that leads to permanent partial paralysis and deformities) and developed an early test for syphilis (an infectious, sexually transmitted disease that if left untreated can cause blindness and insanity).

◢ CLARENCE WALTON LILLEHEI (1918–1999)

American surgeon considered by many to be the "father of open-heart surgery." Thanks to Lillehei's methods and his use of the pacemaker (an instrument that regulates the heartbeat through electrical stimulation), many people with heart conditions once considered fatal have been saved. In 1969, as head of the surgical team at New York Hospital, Lillehei performed the first transplant of a heart and both lungs. He was known as a great teacher, schooling hundreds of doctors in the precise art of heart surgery.

◢ JOSEPH EDWARD MURRAY (1919–)

American surgeon who performed the first successful transplant of an entire human organ—a kidney—from one human being to another. As a young doctor, Murray treated burn victims by grafting healthy skin from one part of a patient's body onto the injured area. He also experimented with grafting skin from other people onto severely burned patients and studied how the body rejected the foreign tissue. He learned that the likelihood of rejection dropped sharply when the donor and patient were related, and he used that discovery in 1954 to successfully transplant a kidney from a live donor into the donor's identical twin brother, who was near death from kidney disease. Murray later tested the drug azathioprine, which prevents the immune system from rejecting transplanted organs, and became the first doctor to transplant kidneys from both unrelated and recently deceased donors.

▲ GEORGE NICHOLAS PAPANICOLAOU (1883–1962)

Greek-American physician and inventor of the Pap smear, a procedure that can detect cancer of the cervix (the constricted, lower end of the uterus) in women. As a researcher at Cornell Medical College in the 1920s, Papanicolaou studied vaginal fluids and found that cancer causes changes in cells even in its earliest stages. The Pap smear today is an inexpensive screening test given to women at their yearly gynecological examinations. It allows physicians to diagnose cervical cancer when the disease is at its most treatable stage and is considered one of the greatest life-saving techniques in the history of medicine.

▲ ALBERT BRUCE SABIN (1906–1993)

Polish-American microbiologist best known for developing the oral (taken by mouth) vaccine for polio. Sabin's vaccine, produced in 1957 and approved for use in the United States in 1960, consisted of live, weakened strains of the polio virus. The oral vaccine was an improvement on the earlier shot form developed by Jonas Salk (1914–1995; see box on page 202) because it is easier to give and results in stronger, longer-lasting immunity. Sabin actively lobbied for his vaccine to be given to children in poorer nations.

Albert Sabin.
(Courtesy of the Library of Congress.)

▲ HENRY E. SIGERIST (1891–1957)

Swiss-American physician and a founder of the discipline of scientific history. Sigerist documented the history and development of medicine, as well as its effect on patients, doctors, and society. He stressed the humanitarian ideal that medicine should serve the needs of all people equally. Sigerist is best remembered for his monumental book *History of Medicine* (1951–1961). He also wrote several other books, including *Great Doctors* (1933), *Medicine and Human Welfare* (1941), *Civilization and Disease* (1943), and *Socialized Medicine in the Soviet Union* (1937).

▲ MARIE CARMICHAEL STOPES (1880–1958)

British health-care advocate, botanist, and writer who opened the first birth control clinic in Great Britain and championed the right of women to use contraception (see essay Issues and Developments in Birth Control in this chapter). Between 1921 and 1977, when Stopes operated a series of women's reproductive clinics, she faced opposition from legislators, medical personnel, and especially the Catholic Church (which opposes artificial birth control). Stopes was also criticized by others in the reproductive freedom and women's rights movements for stating that people she considered "unfit" for parenthood—such as drug addicts, criminals, people of mixed race, and people with mental illnesses—should be sterilized (undergo a surgical procedure that makes them unable to bear children).

▲ HELEN BROOKE TAUSSIG (1898–1986)

American physician who founded the field of pediatric cardiology (the study of heart disease in children). Taussig and a colleague, surgeon Alfred Blalock (1899–1964), developed a procedure for treating newborns with "blue baby" syndrome (a condition in which a heart defect prevents the blood from getting enough oxygen and makes the skin appear blue). The procedure, which involves repairing or attaching an artery in the heart or lungs, has saved the lives of thousands of children. Taussig became the first female full professor at Johns Hopkins Medical School in 1959. After her retirement she fought for the humane treatment of laboratory animals and a woman's right to abortion.

▲ JULIUS WAGNER-JUAREGG (1857–1940)

Austrian psychiatrist and pioneer of unusual techniques of treating mental illness and partial paralysis brought on by advanced syphilis (an infectious, sexually transmitted disease that if left untreated can cause blindness and insanity). Wagner-Juaregg's most famous treatment involved causing fever by infecting syphilis patients with malaria (a disease, spread by mosquitoes, characterized by fever, chills, and sweating). He found that many patients showed considerable improvement after episodes of high fever. Wagner-Juaregg then cured the patients of malaria using the drug quinine. Malaria treatment became a standard procedure for syphilis patients until the penicillin and other antibiotics became widely available after World War II (1939–45; see essay The Discovery, Importance, and Limitations of Antibiotics in this chapter).

▲ THOMAS HUCKLE WELLER (1915–)

American physician, virologist (a scientist who studies viruses), and bacteriologist (a scientist who studies bacteria) whose greatest contribution to medicine was the discovery that the polio-causing virus could be cultivated in a test tube (polio is a disease, often affecting children, that leads to permanent, partial paralysis and deformities). Weller's discovery was a necessary first step toward the mass-production of the polio vaccine, a serum that uses live or killed strains of the virus. For his achievement Weller won the Nobel Prize in physiology or medicine in 1954.

◢ PAUL MAURICE ZOLL (1911–1999)

American cardiologist (a heart doctor) who conducted research that led to the development of the cardiac pacemaker (an instrument that regulates heartbeat through electrical stimulation) in 1952. Zoll also pioneered the use of heart monitors (instruments that monitor heart activity) and countershock defibrillators (machines that can restart a heart through electrical stimulation) on heart patients. Zoll conducted medical research at Beth Israel Hospital and Harvard Medical School, both in Boston, and served as a consultant in cardiology to several other Boston hospitals.

RESEARCH AND ACTIVITY IDEAS

(1) Abortion, the expulsion or removal of an embryo or fetus from the womb, was legalized in 1973 by the U.S. Supreme Court in a case called *Roe v. Wade*. Since that time, a lengthy and heated struggle over abortion has been fought in the United States. On one side are people who consider abortion immoral and essentially murder and wish to see it outlawed; on the other side are people who view abortion as a woman's right to control her body and life and believe that it should remain legal. Form two teams of students, with one team representing each side of the struggle, and research the arguments. Then hold a debate on the topic.

(2) Polio, an infectious viral disease that leads to permanent, partial paralysis and deformities, was one of the most feared childhood diseases in the 1950s. Many medical researchers during that period worked to develop a polio vaccine. By the end of the 1950s there were two available: one created by Jonas Salk (1914–1995) that used the killed form of the virus and was given by injection, and one created by Albert Sabin (1906–1993) that used live strains of the virus and was given by mouth. Due to widespread vaccination campaigns in the United States, the incidence of polio had fallen by 96 percent by the year 1961; today it is almost nonexistent. Write a research

paper on the history of polio in the United States and how the disease was eliminated.

(3) AIDS, which stands for acquired immunodeficiency syndrome, was first diagnosed in 1981. In the United States, the population most affected by AIDS was homosexual males. (In Africa, where roughly 70 percent of AIDS victims live today, the disease is most common in sexually active heterosexuals and affects women and men in equal numbers.) Because AIDS was labeled a "gay disease," many social critics argue, the disease has not received the research dollars it deserves, slowing progress toward finding a vaccine or a cure. The controversy over spending on AIDS research sparked an AIDS protest movement, rooted in the gay and lesbian community. Research and write about the groups involved in AIDS research advocacy, and outline their concerns and demands.

(4) When penicillin was invented, it was seen as a "miracle drug" for its ability to cure what had previously been considered life-threatening conditions. The drug, first mass-produced in British factories in 1942, saved the lives of countless combatants in World War II (1939–45) who might have otherwise died from infections. Write about or prepare an oral presentation on the story of penicillin, starting with Scottish bacteriologist (a scientist who studies bacteria) Alexander Fleming (1881–1955), who accidentally discovered the anti-bacterial properties of bread mold growing in his lab and continuing through the development of the drug for human use by Australian-English pathologist (a scientist who studies diseases) Howard Florey (1898–1968) and German biochemist (a scientist who studies the chemistry of living things) Ernst Chain (1906–1979).

(5) Prepare an oral presentation that answers the following questions about cancer and smoking: When were tobacco products first linked to cancer? When was it determined that tobacco companies had been concealing evidence that their products were dangerous to human health? How did tobacco companies make cigarettes more addictive? What has been the result of the U.S. Food and Drug Administration's (FDA) decision to regulate tobacco products as drugs? How have smoking rates among youth changed over the past ten years?

(6) As the success rates of organ transplants have steadily increased, demand for organs has greatly outpaced supply. In response, health officials have mounted educational campaigns to persuade people to sign up as organ donors in the event of their death. Visit the Web site

of the United Network for Organ Sharing at http://www.unos.org to learn more about organ donation. Then produce a leaflet to circulate at your school that supports organ donation and informs people about how to become organ donors.

⑦ The World Health Organization (WHO) is a program of the United Nations that conducts vaccination and health education campaigns in the developing world and helps countries establish public health services. Visit the WHO Web site at http://www.who.int/home-page/ and read about the organization's various programs. Choose the program that most interests you and write a report about it.

FOR MORE INFORMATION

Books

Altman, Linda Jacobs. *Plague and Pestilence: A History of Infectious Disease.* Springfield, NJ: Enslow Publishers, Inc., 1998.

Bell, Allison. *Your Body, Yourself: A Guide to Your Changing Body.* Los Angeles: A Lowell House Book, 1993.

Benowitz, Steven I. *Cancer.* Berkeley Heights, NJ: Enslow Publishers, Inc., 1999.

Bredeson, Carmen. *Jonas Salk: Discoverer of the Polio Vaccine.* Hillside, NJ: Enslow Publishers, Inc., 1993.

Caplan, Arthur, and Daniel Coelho, eds. *The Ethics of Organ Transplants: The Current Debate.* New York: Prometheus, 1999.

Check, William A. *AIDS.* Philadelphia, PA: Chelsea House Publishers, 1999.

Gallo, Robert C. *Virus Hunting—AIDS, Cancer, and the Human Retrovirus, a Story of Scientific Discovery.* New York: BasicBooks, 1991.

Gottfried, Ted. *Alexander Fleming: Discoverer of Penicillin.* New York: Franklin Watts, 1997.

Growing Up: Eating for Health. Chicago: World Book, Inc., 1993.

Hyde, Margaret O., and Elizabeth H. Forsyth. *Vaccinations: From Smallpox to Cancer.* New York: Franklin Watts, 2000.

Kaye, Judith. *The Life of Florence Sabin.* New York: Twenty-First Century Books, 1993.

Kittredge, Mary. *Organ Transplants.* Philadelphia: Chelsea House Publishers, 2000.

Koven, Edward L. *Smoking: The Story Behind the Haze.* New York: Nova Science Publishers, 1996.

Kronstadt, Janet. *Florence Sabin: Medical Researcher.* New York: Chelsea House Publishers, 1990.

Majure, Janet. *AIDS.* Springfield, NJ: Enslow Publishers, 1998.

McGlashan, Agnes M., and Christopher J. Reeve. *Sigmund Freud: Founder of Psychoanalysis.* New York: Praeger Publishers, 1970.

McPherson, Stephanie Sammartino. *The Workers' Detective: A Story About Dr. Alice Hamilton.* Minneapolis, MN: Carolrhoda Books, 1992.

Mulcahy, Robert. *Medical Technology: Inventing the Instruments.* Minneapolis, MN: The Oliver Press, Inc., 1997: 73–88.

Nash, Carol Rust. *AIDS: Choices for Life.* Springfield, NJ: Enslow Publishers, 1997.

Rubin, Eva R. *The Abortion Controversy: A Documentary History.* Westport, CT: Greenwood Press, 1994.

Saari, Peggy and Stephen Allison, eds. *Scientists: The Lives and Works of 150 Scientists,* Vol. 3. Farmington Hills, MI: U•X•L, 1996: 882–888.

Silverstein, Alan, Virginia Silverstein, and Laura Silverstein Nunn. *AIDS: An All-About Guide for Young Adults.* Springfield, NJ: Enslow Publishers, 1999.

Simmons, Alex. *Ben Carson.* Austin, TX: Raintree Steck-Vaughn, 1996.

Terkel, Susan Neiburg and Marlene Lupiloff-Brazz. *Understanding Cancer.* New York: Franklin Watts, 1993.

Travers, Bridget, and Fran Locher Freiman, eds. *Medical Discoveries: Medical Breakthroughs and the People Who Developed Them.* Farmington Hills, MI: U•X•L, 1997.

Vitkus, Jessica, and Marjorie Ingall. *Smart Sex.* New York: Pocket Books, 1998.

Yount, Lisa. *Medical Technology.* New York: Facts on File, Inc., 1998: 112–130.

Periodicals

Altman, Lawrence K. "Christiaan Barnard, 78, Surgeon for First Heart Transplant, Dies." *The New York Times.* September 3, 2001: A1.

Colen, B. D. "Organ Concert: By Playing Just the Right Keys, Scientists Hope to Lull the Body's Immune System Into Accepting Selected Foreigners Into the Neighborhood." *Time.* Fall 1996 (vol. 148, no. 14): 70+.

Golden, Frederic. "Patrick Steptoe and Robert Edwards: Brave New Baby Doctors." *Time.* March 29, 1999: 178.

Langreth, Robert. "Outsmarting AIDS." *Forbes.* September 17, 2001: 160.

"Officials Voice Alarm Over Halt in AIDS Decline." *The New York Times.* August 14, 2001: A13.

Pesta, Jesse, and Mark Schoofs. "A Crucible for Generic AIDS Medicines—Tests of Drugs in Nigeria, India May Well Shape the Destiny of Millions." *The Wall Street Journal.* August 2, 2001: A10.

"The Pill That Transformed America." *Newsweek.* Winter 1997 (vol. 130, no. 24-A): 76.

"The Puzzle People: Memoirs of a Transplant Surgeon" (book review). *Publishers Weekly.* June 29, 1992: 44.

Stearns, Richard D. "Mercy Impaired." *Christianity Today.* September 3, 2001: 100.

Web sites

"10 Notable Jefferson Alumni of the Past: John H. Gibbon Jr." *Thomas Jefferson University.* http://jeffline.tju.edu/SML/archives/exhibits/notable_alumni/john_gibbon_jr.html (accessed April 8, 2002).

"Alexis Carrel." *DISCovering Science.* Gale Research, 1996. Reproduced in Discovering Collection. Farmington Hills, MI: Gale Group. December 2000. http://www.galenet.com/servlet/DC/ (accessed April 8, 2002).

"Alexis Carrel—Biography." *Nobel e-Museum.* http://www.nobel.se/medicine/laureates/1912/carrel-bio.html (accessed April 8, 2002).

"Alice Hamilton." *Distinguished Women of Past and Present.* http://www.distinguishedwomen.com/biographies/hamilton-a.html (accessed April 8, 2002).

"Alice Hamilton, M.D." *National Institute of Occupational Safety and Health.* http://www.cdc.gov/niosh/hamhist.html#person (accessed April 8, 2002).

American Cancer Society Home Page. http://www.cancer.org/ (accessed April 8, 2002).

"Antibiotics." *U•X•L Science.* U•X•L, 1998. Reproduced in Discovering Collection. Farmington Hills, MI: Gale Group. December 2000. http://www.galenet.com/servlet/DC/ (accessed April 8, 2002).

"Benjamin Carson." *U•X•L Biographies.* U•X•L, 1999. Reproduced in Discovering Collection. Farmington Hills, MI: Gale Group. December 2000. http://www.galenet.com/servlet/DC/ (accessed April 8, 2002).

"Benjamin Carson, M.D." *Johns Hopkins Medicine Department of Neurosurgery.* http://www.neuro.jhmi.edu/profiles/carson.html (accessed April 8, 2002).

"Florence Sabin." *The Architect of the Capitol.* http://www.aoc.gov/cc/art/nsh/sabin.htm (accessed April 8, 2002).

"Florence R. Sabin." *National Academy of Sciences.* http://www.nationalacademies.org/history/members/sabin.html (accessed April 8, 2002).

"Gibbon Develops the Heart-Lung Machine, 1934." *DISCovering U.S. History.* Gale Research, 1997. Reproduced in Discovering Collection.

Farmington Hills, MI: Gale Group. December 2000. http://www.galenet.com/servlet/DC/ (accessed April 8, 2002).

"In vitro fertilization." *U•X•L Science.* U•X•L, 1998. Reproduced in Discovering Collection. Farmington Hills, MI: Gale Group. December 2000. http://www.galenet.com/servlet/DC/ (accessed April 8, 2002).

"HIV/AIDS Research Agenda and Fact Sheets." *NIAID Home Page.* http://www.niaid.nih.gov (accessed April 8, 2002).

O'Malley, Martin, Owen Wood, and Amy Foulkes. "Backgrounder: The Pill and Us." *CBC News Online.* http://www.cbc.ca/news/indepth/background/birthcontrol_pill.html (accessed April 8, 2002).

Planned Parenthood Federation of America. http://www.plannedparenthood.org (accessed April 8, 2002).

"Public Health Service Established, 1912." *DISCovering U.S. History.* Gale Research, 1997. Reproduced in Discovering Collection. Farmington Hills, MI: Gale Group. December 2000. http://www.galenet.com/servlet/DC/ (accessed April 8, 2002).

Sigmund Freud and the Freud Archives. http://users.rcn.com/brill/freudarc.html (accessed April 8, 2002).

"Staff: Robert C. Gallo." *Institute of Human Virology.* http://www.ihv.org/pages/about/about_staff_gallo.htm (accessed April 8, 2002).

Thomas E. Starzl Transplantation Institute. http://www.sti.upmc.edu/ (accessed April 8, 2002).

United Network for Organ Sharing (UNOS). http://www.unos.org (accessed April 8, 2002).

United States Public Health Service. http://www.hhs.gov/phs/ (accessed April 8, 2002).

World Health Organization. http://www.who.int/home-page/ (accessed April 8, 2002).

Index

I

J